The COACH GAITHER *Story*

Strong Faith and Tough Love in the Star City

D1253710

BY TED EDLICH WITH BARRY BROWN

TESTIMONIALS

I have seen Coach Gaither take the toughest young man, angry at himself and the world, and turn him around into a different person, with hope for the future and a willingness to work hard. Of course, he had an unmatchable winning record with our team. However, it was more than that. His incredibly positive presence impacted our entire school. There is no one I respect more than Joe Gaither as a man, coach, and educator.

Alyce Szathmary, *former principal, William Fleming High School*

Joe Gaither could make you believe that outstanding achievement, that being the best, is as likely as taking your next breath. He had the gift of true leadership. Looking back on those moments reminds me that, because of Coach, I had developed an almost irrational confidence that I could be on a team of winning players in the greatest of contests. That is the gift I have tried to pass on to my former players at the Golden State Warriors and my present teams at the University of California Irvine.

Russell Turner, *head men's basketball coach, University of California, Irvine*

Coach Gaither had a tough-love approach that was stern but compassionate. I always knew he wanted the best for me and my family. He was the kind of coach you just didn't want to let down because you knew he cared about you and genuinely wanted what was best for you in life. He called his players "son" because he treated them as such.

Tarik Turner, *college basketball studio and game analyst for FOX Sports*

Coach Joe has been in my life since I was fourteen, and I'm fifty-one now. Joe is dear to my heart, part of my family, and part of my life. I'm proud to be a branch of his coaching tree.

Jason Nibblet, *Girls Basketball Coach, Carlisle School*

Of course, Joe wanted us to be competitive. But he wanted more from his players. He wanted us to compete with grace and dignity. Why? Because the world does not expect grace and dignity from young Black men. He always reminds us that the way we conducted ourselves reflected on us, on him, on our parents, and our community.

Tony Joyce, *former player, insurance company manager*

When I've coached basketball, I have continued what I have learned from Coach Gaither, especially discipline and accountability. Young people respond to those values as long as they know that you also care about them personally, aside from their performance on the court. A sense of playfulness is also important to soften the impact when we all make mistakes no matter how hard we try. This was the foundation that I learned from Joe Gaither. Others have built on that foundation. However, nothing replaces that foundation.

Curtis Blair, *NBA referee*

This book is absolutely stunning—way beyond an excellent biography. It captures the strength and passion of Coach Gaither, brings to life on every page his intelligence, talent, vision, leadership, and faith, and most of all, his deep, caring soul.

Anna Lawson, *Ph.D., former Chair of Board of Trustees, Hollins University*

This book is dedicated to the legacy and memory of my dear mother, Laura Holland Gaither, my loving wife Bernice, my sons James and Michael, and my mentor Paul "Creedy" Moyer. Above all, I pray that my Lord Jesus Christ be glorified by this story.

–Joe Gaither

"But by the grace of God, I am what I am."

I CORINTHIANS 15:10

TABLE OF CONTENTS

FOREWORD

By Steve Bowery, Heywood Fralin, and Curtis Staples

STEVE BOWERY

The message on the phone began, "Hey, Steve. It's me, Joe. There is something I've been working on, and I want to share it with you. I need your help." I have been getting those messages frequently over the last 25 years. The "something" varied.

The first "something" came during Joe's successful tenure as a coach and mentor for poor Black kids through the Inner City Athletic Association. The somethings continued through his 13 years of coaching AAU basketball at the highest national levels—creating opportunities for area youngsters to test their athleticism and character against the very best—and as Joe's protégés needed help finding athletic scholarships and preparing for academic success on their way to adult careers.

As years went by, the somethings would involve projects for Shiloh Baptist Church in Salem, Virginia, where Joe served as deacon. They would involve projects for Straight Street (a Christian outreach program to promote a safe place and healthy activities for young people), the Fellowship of Christian Athletes, and the Roanoke Kiwanis organization. All these organizations have benefited from Coach Joe's drive and passion to improve the lives of others.

A couple of years ago, Joe's friend and work colleague, Barry Brown, proposed a biography to showcase all that Joe had done throughout his life in service to others. The match that Barry lit caught fire. It was a book begging to be written and a story demanding to be told. It drew others into the flame. Ted Edlich, then Dave Russo, joined the writing team. A small group of us reached out to others who had also provided financial support to Coach Joe's efforts and raised the additional funds needed to bring on the talents of a first-class editor, Emily Kincer, and our graphic designer, Kelly Stanley, to ensure that the book merited Joe Gaither's name on the cover.

When I got to read the finished manuscript, it was more than I had anticipated. Until I read about Joe's family and his ancestors, I did not know the whole Joe Gaither. The story is more than a sports story, though it is a great sports story. It is more than a story about mentoring, though it is a great story of a first-class mentor. It is a story that sets all of us in a historical context that challenges us, raises questions, and brings us to a greater appreciation of each other. Once I began reading *The Coach Gaither Story*, I could not put it down. It is an awesome read.

Getting back to those recurring voicemails over the last 25 years, the miracle is that I kept calling back. I knew that there was going to be an ask. And I knew that I was not going to be able to turn him down. Yet, I always called back asking about the new project that had him so excited, and what it would cost to make it happen. In the end, I have never found myself poorer by answering his call. Indeed, I have felt blessed, just like the young people he has helped. I have become richer, not poorer, from helping Coach Joe Gaither further his mission.

My hope is that this biography of the man we have come to love will touch you as deeply as he has touched us.

–Steve Bowery
Principal and Portfolio Manager, Wilbanks Smith & Thomas
Asset Management, LLC, Roanoke, Virginia

HEYWOOD FRALIN

My relationship with Joe Gaither began almost 20 years ago. Some of my friends in the Roanoke business community at the time told me about Joe, describing him as a person that I ought to meet because he was having a great influence on the kids living in underserved communities in Roanoke.

Following the suggestion, I attended an Inner City Athletic Association event where Joe described his efforts. I began to follow the activities of ICAA and observe the significantly positive impact Joe was having on this community. I soon came to realize that Joe was a man of great substance and depth. We began to see more and more of each other, eventually becoming close friends.

There is a quote from Winston Churchill that goes a long way in describing the life and mission of Joe Gaither:

> The destiny of mankind is not decided by material computation. When great causes are on the move in the world... we learn that we are spirits, not animals, and that something is going on in space and time, and beyond space and time, which whether we like it or not, spells duty.

Churchill of course was referring to World War II. In Joe's case, this quote speaks to his mission to help underprivileged children—most of whom are living in poverty—secure a meaningful life through education and mentorship created in a sports setting.

Make no mistake, when Coach Joe leads young men to the court or field, he wants to win and expects maximum effort from all players. While his teams are usually successful, Joe's life is not about success—it is about significance. Joe's wins in sports are rewarding, but for him, the only true significance comes from changing the lives of young people so they ultimately become well-rounded, successful, and educated parents leading the next generation to play a meaningful role in society.

There are not many Joe Gaithers in our troubled world. It has been gratifying for me to be able to call such a special human being a good friend.

-Heywood Fralin
Businessman and philanthropist, Roanoke, Virginia

CURTIS STAPLES

The Coach Gaither Story provides an in-depth look at Joe's tireless commitment to the community and especially the youth in the inner-city of Roanoke, Virginia, throughout an over 40-year span through mentorship and coaching. As we all know, being a great coach is not just about a sport's X's and O's. It is also about the ability to bring the most out of a person, more than they thought they were capable of or could ever imagine.

Joe Gaither consistently inspired and instilled confidence in his players year after year by stressing the importance of dedication and preparation.

When I was 12 years old, I joined the Inner City Athletic Association (ICAA) as a youth football player and met Coach Joe Gaither for the first time. I had been previously committed to the youth program at the local YMCA, but I became curious after two years as to why and how the players at ICAA were so consistently dominant. My father, Bruce Staples, finally allowed me to try out for the ICAA football program after I begged him all summer long. This football team became more than just a recreational sport that won championships. It was the start of a lifelong relationship that showed unwavering loyalty, commitment to being the best at a sport, and most important, it was the start of learning what my true purpose in life was meant to be—which is my walk with my Lord and Savior Jesus Christ, to which Coach Joe personally guided me in knowledge and understanding.

You will hear from many players in this book who will share memorable moments of their time with Coach Joe. I'm sure that one of the common things that will stick out throughout their stories will be the amount of undeniable success that was achieved while playing for Coach Joe. They will all speak about the hard practices to prepare for the opposition and the strict level of respect demanded while competing. Coach Joe not only taught all his youth how to dominate on the field and the court; he also taught the importance of having manners and being a well-rounded and respectful young man. He demanded that every response to a question from an adult, man or a woman, be answered with a "yes, ma'am" or a "yes, sir." Any other response was unacceptable.

For most youth, Coach Joe was seen as their father due to not having a biological one at home. But for some like myself, Coach Joe was a constant reinforcement of the beliefs that were vehemently stressed at the home front. Parents knew that by allowing their sons to play for Joe Gaither, they could trust that their child would not only be taught the tangible skills to assist them in becoming a successful athlete but also have the comfort of knowing that their son was learning about becoming a productive citizen in society.

While every child under Coach Joe's tutelage didn't grasp all the knowledge he bestowed upon them, many like myself took full advantage of their time with him. As you will read, Coach Joe would become personally responsible for hundreds of student-athletes accepting college scholarships to play at Division I and Division II schools and universities, as well as watching a handful of his protégés compete in the professional ranks as players and eventually as coaches as their playing careers came to an end.

I feel the luckiest of them all, as Coach Joe has continued to remain the most important part of my professional coaching career, still coaching alongside me after more than a decade. His legacy continues to help shape young men and communities to live a life of service, humility, and honor.

–Curtis Staples
Director of Advancement, Lakeway Christian Schools,
White Pines, Tennessee

Joe Gaither with Curtis
Staples when the
University of Virginia
retired Curtis's number
5 jersey. Photo by
Bernice Gaither.

INTRODUCTION: MULTIPLE THREADS WITHIN ONE TAPESTRY

The story of Joe Gaither is an incredible tapestry woven from the commanding colors of many vibrant threads. It displays a life born of tragedy, filled with heroism, uplifted by good fortune, and fueled by determination, hard work, hope, and faith.

It is the story of a Black man whose African ancestors were once free Cameroon tribesmen. That is, until they were captured and sold to European slave traders, who, in turn, sold the captives to the burgeoning slave markets of the American colonies.

It is the story of many strong women, none more determined and persistent than Joe's mother, who at 13 was snatched from her Franklin County, Virginia, elementary school and placed into servitude to a White family in another city as the family's cook and housekeeper.

It is the story of a teenage romance that blossomed into a marriage that withstood the traumas of wartime separation and the struggles of earning a living and rearing two talented sons in a segregated society. It is a testament to that 51-year partnership, which was bound by faith, commitment, and love.

It is the story of a Black teacher who urged a young student to develop a talent that ultimately saved his life during the Vietnam War and, back home, led to a secure government job that supported his deepest calling—helping young athletes create a future of promise.

It is the story of a boy whose father abruptly abandoned him and his mother when he was only six years old, who hungered to be mentored by a man of character. It is the story of this child growing into a caring role model for his two sons, his grandchild, and hundreds of other young men.

It is a story of faith—how unbeknownst to us, there is a greater power working in our lives, leading us to the point where we can extend that grace and power to others.

It is also a story of the sport of basketball. Of those who started at the lowest level and were led by a coach who prepared them to play at a level once thought beyond their reach.

COURTSIDE AT THE NATIONAL AAU 17 & UNDER FINALS

The year. 1988. The place: Seattle, Washington. The event: The National AAU 17 & Under Basketball Finals between the two best teams of the hundreds from across the U.S. The game pitted the Roanoke Hawks against the top-seeded Memphis team.

From 1986–1988, the Roanoke Hawks, led by Coach Joe Gaither, dominated AAU basketball in Virginia. This team had won the Virginia 15 & Under AAU Championship in 1986 and went on to win third place in the national tournament. The following year, the Hawks again won the state championship and placed seventh in the national tournament.

By 1988, the Hawks were playing in the 17 & Under league, the team consisting of AAU veterans from within a 50-mile radius centered in Roanoke, Virginia. They were:

- Mark Ward, Alphonso Ward, and Alvin Howard from William Fleming High School;
- George Lynch, Curtis Blair, Bernard Basham, and Russell Turner from Patrick Henry High School;
- Ronald Murphy and Gordon Winn from North Cross High School;
- Jason Niblett from Laurel Park High School;
- Doug Day from Blacksburg High School;
- Jerome Preston from Magna Vista High School; and
- Keith Hamilton from Heritage High School.

The team continued their winning streak, again claiming the state title. To prepare for the national tournament, the Hawks competed with the strongest basketball talent they could find. Joe recalls, "We entered AAU tournaments in North Carolina, West Virginia, and southwest Virginia. We played an extra 29 games against the best competition we could find. In addition, we scrimmaged against college players."

However, the team's preparation hadn't accounted for losing George Lynch, considered by many to be the Hawks' most talented player. During the 1988 Virginia high school basketball season, George led the Patrick Henry High School team in a 28-win and 1-loss season, including winning the state championship. He received Virginia's "Mr. Basketball" award for his performance that year.

George had just enrolled in the prestigious Flint Hill Preparatory Academy, where he was fine-tuning his athletic and academic skills before seeking a top university athletic scholarship. Flint Hill, placing their program first, refused to allow George to fly to Washington to play in any of the national AAU finals games. Alvin Howard also had to drop out at the last minute, placing additional pressure on the remaining players to compensate for his loss.

"Memphis was the top-seeded team in the AAU 17U finals," Joe remembers. "Their point guard, Penny Hardaway, at the age of seventeen, was rated the top high school player in that position in the nation." Confronted by the loss of George and Alvin and the strength of Memphis's talent, the Roanoke Hawks agreed they would not be deterred.

The players had learned two things from their years with Coach Gaither. First, the team that works the hardest in practice has an advantage when game time arrives. "Don't let anyone outwork you. The greatest motivation is perspiration!" became their mantra.

Second, you cannot worry about what or who you don't have. Instead, take what you do have and make the most of it. In sports and in life, "Your will must be greater than your skill. Your reach must exceed your grasp."

Recalling the night before the game that would determine the number one AAU team in the nation, Joe comments:

> I didn't get much sleep that night. Previously, we won our last game against the Arkansas Wings in the semifinals by a very close margin. Had the Hawks' Doug Day not come up with 27 points from the field and then made two foul shots to put us in overtime, the Arkansas Wings rather than the Roanoke Hawks would be facing Memphis in the finals. In overtime, the Roanoke Hawks won the semifinals by a few points—a close one! Tomorrow, we had to play even better against Memphis, the number one seed in the nation.

The next morning, Joe, surrounded by his team, began by giving thanks to the Lord for all who had contributed to that day. In that prayer, he gave special attention to his players. "These young men remain the greatest examples I have seen in overcoming obstacles and reaching down inside themselves for excellence," he recalls saying. He also added special thanks to community business leaders who had championed the Hawks' program by sponsoring the team's flights, lodging, and meals during the seven-day event.

At game time, Coach Gaither took in the whole scene. The stands were packed with fans, family, and locals. The first two rows—on all sides of the gym—were filled with collegiate talent scouts from across the nation, seeking the best student-athletes for their institutions.

After the usual introductions of the two teams, comments by the head of the AAU national committee, and the beginning toss-up, the game was on. It was a two-point game all the way to the final moments of the last quarter. The lead constantly transferred between the Hawks and Memphis, with neither team breaking away from the other by a large margin.

Finally, with 3 minutes and 47 seconds to go in the fourth quarter, the Roanoke Hawks broke away with an 8-point lead. Suddenly, point guard Penny Hardaway called for a timeout. Both teams surrounded their coaches in front of their respective benches. From the corner of his eye, Joe saw Hardaway slap one of the players in the Memphis huddle and scream out to his teammates, "You better not quit!" Within less than four minutes, Hardaway and Memphis took over and tied the score, putting the game in overtime. Memphis closed with a more convincing margin than they had managed throughout the entire game.

Joe reminisces on that moment:

> We played our hearts out. In the remaining time, Memphis tied us and then took the title in overtime, 84 to 76. I cannot say enough about our team. The Hawks may have lost that game, but we were also winners. We were the second-best AAU team in the nation with talent that had come not from an entire state but a 50-mile radius around the City of Roanoke, Virginia. Every Hawks player gave his very best effort.
>
> We also witnessed one of the greatest basketball players and court leaders of our time, Penny Hardaway, who, after playing for the University of Memphis, was drafted by the Orlando Magic and had a stellar career playing alongside the great Shaq O'Neal.

Upon their return to Roanoke, the Hawks were awarded the Key to the City. "I will never forget the honor I feel, to this day, of having the opportunity to work with such a courageous group of young men, who again and again defied the odds to win for their team," states Joe. "All of the players went on to play Division I college basketball or football. They have continued to represent our Roanoke Valley and the Commonwealth of Virginia with their courage, hard work, and dedication to be the best."

Roanoke Councilman Jim Trout presents the Key to the City to Roanoke Hawks' Coach Joe Gaither. The team had just landed at Woodrum Field after winning second place in the national AAU tournament for players 17-and-under. Photo by Dan Doughtie for The Roanoke Times.

WILLIAM JOSEPH GAITHER AND HIS AFRICAN ROOTS

On June 4, 1949, William Joseph Gaither was born at Burrell Memorial Hospital in the historic Black community of Gainesboro in Roanoke, Virginia.

Laura Gaither with Joe, 1949.

Placing the newborn's life in historical perspective, his birth took place:

- Roughly four years after the end of WWII.
- One year after President Harry Truman issued Executive Order 9981 abolishing segregation in the U.S. Armed Services.
- 86 years after President Lincoln's Emancipation Proclamation freed millions of enslaved people and sent the message that they were fully—instead of three-fourths—human beings, entitled to vote in American elections and afforded the protection of the Bill of Rights.
- Nine years before the Supreme Court outlawed segregation in the nation's public schools.
- 15 years before the Civil Rights Act of 1964 prohibited discrimination based on race, color, religion, sex, or national origin.
- 16 years before the 1965 Voting Rights Act, which made good on the 1863 promise of the fundamental right to participate in the nation's democracy.
- 330 years since the first enslaved Africans were brought to the shores of the United States of America, which created a rigid caste system based on the color of one's skin, with Whites, the Brahmin equivalents, at the top, and Blacks, the American "untouchables," at the bottom.[1]

If you are White in America, you can often trace your ancestors beyond their immigration to the United States to their forbearers on foreign soil. If you are Black, it is almost impossible to know your ancestors by name and from what specific country they were abducted, leaving the day of enslavement as the known beginning of the family

---

1   Isabel Wilkerson's comparison of the American racial caste system with the caste systems of India and Nazi Germany is detailed in her book *Caste*. Wilkerson also notes that legal slavery lasted 246 years in America, and if Blacks in America were to have the same number of years in legal freedom, it would take until 2111 for that to have happened.

history. That's why William Holland's discovery of his family's roots in the African nation of Cameroon is so unusual and intriguing.[2]

William, a former Coca-Cola executive, is Joe's cousin. William's dad, Sam Holland, and Joe's mother, Laura Holland, were twins. Brother and sister were born in 1927 to George Holland, a sharecropper in Franklin County, after the fall of Reconstruction and the arrival of the Jim Crow plan of "Southern Redemption" to ensure that the inequalities of slavery were preserved in post-Civil War America.

According to William, his father was passionate about knowing something about their family heritage beyond slavery, years of discrimination, and the psychological trauma Black Americans endured. "Dad said, 'I want to do something. You have the education now. We couldn't say anything at the time, but you can now,'" he recalled to Courtney Cutright of *The Roanoke Times*. That challenge began William's decade-long journey through volumes of ancestral records, DNA testing results and research, and multiple visits to the Cameroon nation and its leadership.[3]

Thanks to the extensive ancestral research and DNA evidence collected by William, there is strong evidence that his and Joe's forbearers included African people captured by ethnic groups in Cameroon and transported to America on European slave ships.[4]

In his travels to Cameroon, the Mankon tribe—who played a role in the slave trade of the 18th century—was the first group with whom William connected. As he explained to Alan Boyle of NBC News, "Mankon didn't trade their own people, but they were the middlemen for people [from other tribes] going down the coast...."[5] The Europeans provided the incentives of alcohol and guns to the tribes as rewards for the abduction and sale of their fellow Africans.[6]

2   Cutright, Courtney. "Reconnecting with his roots: William Holland's Franklin County family reunion included a Cameroon royal family to which he has traced his lineage." The Roanoke Times, n.d., sec. Virginia.
3   Ibid.
4   Boyle, Alan. "African-American's Roots Revised." NBC News, May 14, 2012. https://www.nbcnews.com/science/cosmic-log/african-americans-roots-revised-flna771737.
5   Ibid.
6   Ibid.

William also met with members of the Oku tribe, who confirmed there was a time in the 1770s when scores of their kin were abducted by rival tribes and sold to slave traders.[7] He learned of a widely respected Oku tribe member in the 1700s named Bailack. Many of Bailack's "'several wives and scores of sons...were abducted and passed on to the European slavers during the reign of a ruthless [Mankon] named Ney."[8] Ney, the tribal leader, feared that Bailack's family sought to overthrow his regime, giving him a pretext to abduct and sell them to European slavers.[9]

William's research revealed the likelihood that one of Bailack's family members was brought to Virginia by a slave ship called The Fox in 1772. Stripped of his African name and renamed Glascow, he was purchased by wealthy landowners and transported to Bedford County. Glascow's grandson, Stephen, was purchased by the Holland family, who were plantation owners in Franklin County. Stephen, in turn, was William's great-great-grandfather.[10] William had already established through ancestral records that Creed Holland, who had driven a wagon for the Confederate Army, was his great-grandfather.[11]

The combined evidence of the Holland family's connection to their Cameroon forbearers was strong enough to convince present-day Cameroon leadership of Cameroon's complicity in American slavery. As a result, when representatives from the Cameroon nation traveled to Franklin County to meet with their American descendants, they also signed an apology for Cameroon's involvement in American slavery.[12]

---

7   Ibid.
8   Ibid.
9   Holland, William. "From Royalty to Captive, and Back to Cameroon." Cameroon Traveler Magazine, May 5, 2013. https://cameroontraveler. com/2013/05/05/from-royalty-to-captive-and-back-to-cameroon/.
10 Ibid.
11 Boyle, Alan. "African-American's Roots Revised." NBC News, May 14, 2012. https://www.nbcnews.com/science/cosmic-log/african-americans-roots-revised-flna771737.
12 Boyle, Alan. "Genetic Quest Leads to African Apology for Role in Slave Trade." NBC News, October 27, 2013. https://www.nbcnews.com/sciencemain/genetic-quest-leads-african-apology-role-slave-trade-8C11467842.

Gathering of African Americans and Africans at Franklin County Recreational Park in Virginia to celebrate the Holland family's royal Cameroon heritage. Photo by Bernice Gaither, July 4, 2014.

LAURA HOLLAND,
JOE GAITHER'S MOTHER

The descendants of enslaved people in the United States frequently adopted the surnames of their owners. In Franklin County, Virginia, those bought by the Holland family adopted the "Holland" brand. Such was the case for George Holland and his wife, whose forbearers had been slaves, and their twins, Sam and Laura Holland.

When Laura was a girl of 13, her mother died. George remarried but did not anticipate the level of discord that arose between Laura's new stepmother and the strong-willed, defiant teenager. One can imagine the new wife, the new head woman of the house, expecting George's children to automatically submit to her marital authority. To her surprise, Laura was no pushover. The girl had a powerful sense of who she was and refused to fall in line.

It wasn't long before nonstop disagreements and arguments between the two disrupted family life, placing the man of the house in the middle of two angry women, both wanting him to take her side against the other. The verbal arguments eventually escalated and became physical. During one disagreement, Laura reached for a heavy branch from a wood pile and threatened the older woman, who had been chasing her. That time, the stepmother backed off.

After a hard day in the fields working as a sharecropper—trying to scratch a living from the land for his family—George had to come home to the even harder task of dealing with the struggle between the two women, both of whom looked to him to set the other party straight, neither one willing to surrender.

Joe remembers his grandfather, George, as a strong, hard-working, and intelligent man who was able to fix any situation requiring a mechanical solution. However, the ability to bring a peaceful conclusion to the struggle between his independent young daughter and his resentful new wife was clearly not in his toolbox.

Without the opportunity for family therapy or the presence of a neutral mediating party, George's desperate solution to the problem was to have his daughter removed from the scene. He sought the help of Jim Williams, the owner of the land on which he farmed, to devise a solution and put a plan in motion that would end the discord. Jim agreed to help find a place where Laura would be safe—and away from George and his new wife.

Soon after, Jim or a member of his family picked up Laura without prior notice at the end of her Franklin County school day. He abruptly transported her to the Salem, Virginia, home of his sister, Mary Hodges, where Laura would reside and work as the family's domestic housekeeper and cook. With no clear understanding of the trauma imposed by this abduction, Laura's family sent word that she owed a portion of her wages to those back home.

While Laura maintained an outwardly cordial relationship with her Franklin County family, the traumatic wound she had suffered never fully healed. It was a clear example of the generational psychological trauma of Black Americans that Sam referred to in his discussion with his son, William.

Though Mary's daughter Dorothy taught Laura to read and write years later, the young woman's opportunity for a formal education ended the day she was abducted from her school. When Dorothy married Dr. Russo, Laura became the housekeeper for the Russo family and worked a second job to rent her own place.

While there is no compensation for the horrific abuse she experienced in her life because of the American race caste structure, there is some evidence that Laura and Dorothy may have developed a genuine human connection beyond what might be otherwise explained as a Stockholm Syndrome-generated facsimile.

There is an old recording made by the Hodges family's "Uncle Herbert," who fashioned himself as an early Ed Sullivan. Herbert starts the recording by introducing each of the family members who are present. He then hands the mic to the family audience, inviting each member to say a few words. The respondents, who clearly have not had a chance to practice for the occasion, self-consciously reply. The mic is then turned over to Laura, who sings two songs without accompaniment or the slightest hesitancy. Her voice is clear, assured, and perfectly on key with the artistry of a professional singer. The recording suggests anything but a reluctant young woman at a Hodges family gathering.

Family members and townspeople in Salem recall Dorothy and Laura frequently walking side by side, as shown in the next photo.

Laura Gaither and Dorothy Hodges in Salem, Virginia, in the late 1940s. Photo by Herbert Hodges.

Further indicating a genuine endearment, Joe remembers being treated by Dr. Russo as their family doctor when he was ill. He recalls, "Had it not been for Dr. Russo, who signed all of my required athletic physicals, I would not have been able to participate in school sports. Those costs were well beyond what we were able to afford."

Dave Russo, Dorothy's son, explains:

> I can understand why people who did not know Laura and my mother might be skeptical of their relationship. They lived through many incarnations of racism. They didn't live in an "I don't see color" world any more than we do today. But they became close and remained close for most of their lives. My mother had no friend who knew her better, no companion she cared more about than Laura. To me, that is love.

Laura Gaither and Dorothy Hodges Russo in Salem in the late 1990s. Photo by Dave Russo.

After the announcement of Laura's death in 2007, Dave wrote:

> Dear Joe, I am sorry for your loss and for our loss too. Your mother was like a second mother to my brothers and me. Some of my best memories of home have Laura at the heart of them. I hope to carry her strength, her sense of humor, and her love with me always. I'm sure my brothers feel the same.[13]

Dave's wife, Lila Forro, added: "When I married Dave Russo, I received the gift of meeting Laura Gaither. She took me under her loving wing like a daughter, and I will never forget the courage and the energy with which she lived her life."[14]

There is no telling what Laura would have achieved had she not lived under the racial discrimination of a Jim Crow South and had she been protected by child labor laws and continued her education through high school and college. She was intelligent and determined and could adapt to difficult situations. Those characteristics allowed her to manage great psychological pain with grace and then, throughout most of her life, work two jobs and make a good home for herself and her son.

Laura's singing talent and other abilities were nurtured by her African Methodist Episcopal Church family, a primary source of friendship, training, and spiritual strength. Joe also recalls his mother having a talent for growing flowers. She surrounded herself with beauty. She was also a fabulous cook; friends were frequent guests at her table.

Her desire for Joe to do well in school was no doubt strengthened by the educational opportunities abruptly denied her. She supported her son's basketball and football interests and his love for ping-pong. Nevertheless, before Joe could go to the Theron Williams Recreation Center, where he played ball on its dirt courts, his mom had a hard and fast rule: homework came first.

---

13 Legacy.com. "Laura Holland Gaither Obituary (2007) Roanoke Times," November 17, 2007. https://www.legacy.com/us/obituaries/roanoke/name/laura-gaither-obituary?id=29090447.
14 Ibid.

Laura also made it a point for Joe to attend and participate in the life of the church. Even then, she gave him some leeway—no doubt as a result of her own experience as a youngster of being pushed around by adults. Though she was a congregant of the AME church, Laura gave her son permission to attend Salem's Shiloh Baptist Church, where there were more young people with whom he could associate.

Laura's photograph hangs in the fellowship hall of Shiloh Baptist Church in honor of her many years of managing food preparation there.

Picture of Laura Gaither that hangs in the fellowship hall of Shiloh Baptist Church. Photo by Ken Belton.

THE IMPACT OF
AN ABSENT FATHER

Not much is known about Joe's father except the impact of his absence for most of Joe's life. His father deserted him and his mom when Joe was five or six years of age. To this day, he has little memory of his dad. Throughout much of his early years, not having a father in the home was a source of ridicule by his peers. Though Joe remains grateful to the Black men in his church, community, and schools who reached out to him, modeled good values, and mentored him, the void of not having a father in the home remained. The pain and embarrassment of those offhand remarks by so many left an indelible wound on the young man that later shaped his sense of purpose and direction in his life.

We do know that Joe's father was from New York City. Laura was 22 and fully self-supporting when she married. Perhaps she was attracted to the man from the metropolis in the north because he was a potential source of more opportunity than she had ever known. Obviously, her experience with the men in her immediate family had not been encouraging.

Without excusing Joe's father from his responsibility for leaving his wife and child without financial support, the transition from New York City's relative racial openness to the inescapable racial discrimination in the southern city of Roanoke, Virginia, must have been claustrophobic.

In Roanoke City, Black social, business, recreational, and political life was restrained to the four blocks of Henry Street. Furthermore, the Jim Crow denigration of Blacks was evident in the ubiquity of "White Only" signs in public toilets, water fountains, and eating establishments. To a Black man from New York City, the real message would be clear: "You're Not Wanted."

Despite the absence of a father in the home, Laura provided a solid family foundation for her son. In her life, she mirrored the values of hard work, personal achievement, honesty, confidence in the future, and faith. In retrospect, it makes sense that these two pieces of his "life puzzle"— the presence of a strong, dynamic, and caring mother and the absence of a father in the home—would fit together to shape Joe's mission in life. They drove him to reach out to young men, many raised by single moms, and show them how to use their athletic ability and educational opportunity to discover a new world of possibilities through a college education.

HIGH SCHOOL YEARS: G.W. CARVER AND ANDREW LEWIS HIGH

Throughout his high school career, Joe excelled on and off the court. At G.W. Carver High School, he was recognized by the school administration and his peers for his academic and sports leadership. Joe was president of his junior year class and president of the student council.

Joe's Carver High basketball team went undefeated in the regular 1966 season and averaged nearly 100 points per game, finishing second in the state with a 22-1 record. The team also had the opportunity to scrimmage with a mostly White team from Clifton Forge. One Carver player commented: "...this was the first time any of us had played a mostly Whiter team. They had Walter Banks on their team that year, and he was almost seven feet tall. We put the press on them boys the second half, and it was like who let the dogs out."

For his senior year (12 years after the Brown v. Board of Education Supreme Court decision found racially segregated schools unconstitutional), Joe was moved from G.W. Carver to the newly-integrated Andrew Lewis High School. The Roanoke County plan divided the Black students from G.W. Carver among four large, previously White high schools: Andrew Lewis, William Byrd, Cave Spring, and Northside. The transition was made with little planning to help the students successfully navigate their new surroundings and minimize the impact this change would make on their lives.

Students recognized for past athletic, scholastic, and organizational

CHAMPS

STANDING: R. H. Malone, Coach, James Childress, Michael Hylton, Lewis Jeter, William Gaither, Jhue Hamilton, C. D. Harmon, Principal, Malcolm Waldron, Scorer. KNEELING: Perry Taylor, Larry Terry, Joseph Harris, Captain, Royal Jernigan, George Vineyard.

Yearbook photo of the 1966 George Washington Carver basketball team.

leadership found themselves shorn of that recognition. Joe, a top athlete and scholar at Carver, entered an Andrew Lewis High School senior class of 400 students—more than six times larger than the typical senior class of 60 students at Carver High—as a relative unknown.

For Black students, desegregation resulted in significant damage to their social webs and communal support systems of parents, teachers, community leaders, and fellow students committed to the single goal of encouraging every student to gain the highest possible level of education, the gateway to opportunity in a segregated society.

Suddenly gone was the Black teacher who had the same desire for her student's academic success as if he were her own child. Gone was the respect and trust between the White teachers and Black parents that had existed at G.W. Carver. In every Roanoke County high school, Black students found themselves a very small minority among White students—many of whom had been raised with negative stereotypes of Blacks.

It is not surprising that American desegregation of schools had the immediate result of fewer Black students seeking and gaining acceptance to colleges and universities than before desegregation. Many Black students never made it to graduation in the early years.

Looking back, Joe acknowledges the difficulties. There was, at first, the sudden hesitancy of raising a hand to answer a teacher's question for fear of making a mistake before his new classmates who might judge him. There was the loss of prestige that came with his past leadership accomplishments at Carver.

At the same time, this transition had a few bright sides. First, Andrew Lewis was only a short walk from his house in a familiar neighborhood. Further, Joe was an outstanding athlete, sought by White coaches who were well aware of the accomplishments of the Black talent that came their way.

To this day, Joe is indebted to the welcome he received from Coach Dick Miley, who sought him out even before the public was informed of school desegregation plans. Coach Miley reached out to Joe by going to Carver, handing him a pair of basketball training shoes, and assuring him, "You're going to play for us!" One of Coach Miley's gifts was his desire to know as much as he could about his athletes, their home lives, how they were faring in the classroom, their social lives, and their dreams for the future. He also sought their suggestions on how to improve play on the court. As he created scoring plays for each player, he asked them to give the play a name so it would stay on their minds. He was not surprised that Joe would name his scoring play after his girlfriend, "Bernice."

*Yearbook photo of the five starters for the 1967
Andrew Lewis basketball team: Joe Gaither,
Hal Johnston, Roger Holtman, John Givens,
and Fred Genheimer.*

On Senior Night at Andrew Lewis, it was Coach Miley who walked with Joe to center court in place of his mom, who had to work. At the end of the year, Coach Miley, a graduate of Bridgewater College, played an influential role in the offer of a college scholarship for Joe to attend his alma mater.

Few of those going from G.W. Carver to majority-White high schools would have the same advantages as the Black male athletes. Black males with artistic skills in the visual and performing arts were not initially sought out for their potential contribution to the newly desegregated high schools. Further, Black female students weren't recruited for any of the extracurricular activities they had engaged in, like choir and cheerleading. Title IX, the gender equity ruling that guaranteed girls and women the same advantages in athletics and other programs in federally funded public education, was a good six years in the future.

In his senior year at Andrew Lewis, Joe was one of two Black students to make the men's basketball team, where he was an important contributor with an average of 11 points from the field and six rebounds per game.

Joe ultimately did not pursue the Bridgewater College scholarship because he knew little about Bridgewater and sensed that few Black students attended the college. His lack of experience traveling away from his hometown also contributed to the decision to turn down the scholarship. Though Bridgewater was less than two hours from his home, it had seemed to be on the other side of the earth. He would later endeavor to help underprivileged youth broaden their horizons and overcome similar fears.

THREE MORE
CRITICAL INFLUENCES

In addition to his mother's care, three other puzzle pieces profoundly shaped Joe's life.

BERNICE FITZGERALD:
Friend, Wife, and Partner

At the age of 13, young Joe Gaither fell in love with Bernice Fitzgerald. They both attended the all-Black G.W. Carver Elementary, Junior High, and High School until public school integration came to the Roanoke Valley. After the end of school segregation, Joe, who lived in Salem, attended Andrew Lewis High School to complete his senior year. Bernice instead traveled across the Roanoke Valley to William Byrd High School for her junior and senior years. It was a difficult two years for Bernice, made bearable due to her resilience and her supportive two-parent home of McKinley and Lucy Fitzgerald.

The Fitzgeralds championed education. There is a portrait of Bernice's older sister, Virginia Maxine Fitzgerald, in the Roanoke College Administration Building. After being named the 1964 valedictorian of her Carver High class, Virginia became Roanoke College's first full-time Black student and graduate. This racial groundbreaker would earn both a bachelor's and master's degree in psychology and serve as a psychologist in the VA Hospital in Salem, Virginia, until her retirement.

Bernice was also a strong student and active in the Carver

school band, choir, and cheerleading team. She appreciated the encouragement of her math teacher, who gave her special assignments to challenge her. She gave Bernice confidence that if she worked on her projects, she would do well. Bernice also has fond memories of a librarian who was always accessible and supportive.

At the integrated William Byrd High School, life was vastly different from the encouraging atmosphere of G.W. Carver. She remembers the difficulty of mastering the new textbooks at William Byrd, which were more advanced than the outdated texts reserved for Black students at Carver. Suddenly, gone were Bernice's extra-curricular activities—just keeping up with schoolwork was all the unprepared Black students could handle, through no fault of their own. On top of the academics, Black students were confronted with an extremely hostile environment. They were not wanted, with few exceptions, by the White students. Bathroom walls were filled with in-your-face racial taunts and slurs. There were fights every day in the school halls and grounds, instigated by White students.

In addition to student harassment, the school administration's lack of adequate planning added to the desegregation trauma experienced by Black students. No staff member was concerned with how Black students would get to class. Bernice recalls, "It was a 45-minute walk from our neighborhood to the high school. No one in administration seemed to care until someone must have complained. Finally, they sent a bus to pick us up."

Of the 14 Black women who transferred to William Byrd, only four made it to graduation! Bernice was one of the very few who did walk across the graduation stage and receive her high school diploma.

In addition, only a few Black couples who were not from the same area could continue their relationships once they no longer shared a school. Bernice and Joe were one of the few Black couples who survived this difficult period. Joe had to make special arrangements to see Bernice. He used the Valley Transit system to take the bus from Salem to Vinton, where the Black males of Vinton actively discouraged young men from other neighborhoods who were coming to date "their women." The Vinton boys arranged songs and chants to remind the "out-of-towners" of their lack of status when they entered the Vinton town limits.

His persistence paid off. In 1970, Joe and Bernice were married. They have now spent over five decades by each other's sides. Joe remarks, "At Andrew Lewis High School, I named my scoring play 'Bernice.' She is still my winning play after 52 years."

Joe and Bernice Gaither on an Alaska cruise in 2018. Photo by Princess Cruise Lines.

MRS. JULIA HOFFLER:
The Typing Teacher

Another major influence that shaped Joe's life was his G.W. Carver High School typing teacher, Mrs. Julia Hoffler.

In his extraordinary autobiography, *The Ragman's Son,* actor Kirk Douglas credits a high school English teacher for recruiting the strapping high school wrestler for her drama class and introducing him to the world of the theater. The teacher encouraged Douglas to sharpen his stage skills and seek a performing career. Douglas credits that teacher for changing his life by opening him up to the world of dramatic arts and an incredible future in Hollywood.

Similarly, Mrs. Hoffler changed Joe's life when she recognized the young athlete's superior finger coordination and impressed upon him that he had a natural talent for typing. She urged him to practice, and it wasn't long before the basketball guard was an exceptional typist at the top of his class.

Now, it may seem foolish to compare Joe's typing ability to Kirk Douglas's early acting performance as a career and life game-changer until you hear the whole story.

In 1970 during the Vietnam War, 21-year-old Joe was drafted into the Army. The Vietnam conflict eventually led to the deaths of 57,000 American soldiers. Hundreds of thousands suffered physical and mental wounds, scars that would never completely heal.

At the time of his draft, a particular skill set needed in the war effort was in short supply among American troops. The weapon in mind was not an M1 rifle—it was a typewriter. There was a critical need for administrative staff who were high school graduates and could type. Joe's typing skills sent him to Germany as an administrative clerk and specialist, where he would join the 10% of new Army inductees who spent their time in the relative safety of Europe rather than the high-stakes, mine-filled jungles of Vietnam.

It may have been Kirk Douglas's drama teacher who changed his life, but a Black teacher in a segregated G.W. Carver High School saw in young Joe Gaither a talent that dramatically altered the course of his life and, perhaps, even saved it.

THE U.S. ARMY AND GERMANY

In many ways, Joe's military experience was a difficult period—but there's no doubt it helped shape his life in indelible ways. Joe and Bernice were married just before he received his draft notice. After basic training, Bernice joined her husband in his first assignment to Fort Campbell, Kentucky.

The provost of Fort Campbell took a special interest in the newlywed couple, assisting the two with housing and recommending Joe for promotions. When Joe was assigned to serve in Germany, Bernice was pregnant with their first son, Michael. Unfortunately, the young wife and mother did not get to go to Germany. Instead, Bernice returned home to Roanoke. Michael was nearly three years old before his father laid eyes on him.

There was much about being overseas that led Joe to characterize this time as a "dark period." The months and years away from his wife and child were difficult. In addition, the ubiquitous presence of drugs—especially marijuana and hashish, the usage of which was as common as lighting up a cigarette or downing a can of beer—was a constant temptation. Looking back, Joe is hard on himself for sometimes giving in to the temptation and falling short of the values instilled by a mother who raised him at great cost to herself and who expected only the best from her son. On the other hand, Joe's service in the military opened a whole new world for a young man whose globe had been limited to the segregated geography of the Roanoke Valley.

After basic training, Joe realized he was in the best physical condition of his entire life. He could now run a five-mile sprint without breaking a sweat. However, he was growing bored with the monotony of his routine office work. The young soldier found relief in a familiar space: the gym and basketball court. Each day, after eight hours of administrative work, Joe trained with the all-Black military post basketball team that would eventually hold the squadron title against other all-post teams. Joe was a starting guard on that team. The level of competition was extremely high, with at least one player, guard Harold Benion, who was capable of playing at a professional level.

Joe Gaither takes a jump shot in the U.S. Army gym in Stuttgart, Germany, sometime between 1970-72. Photo by PFC Manuel.

During his service in Germany, European basketball teams were able to recruit up to two Americans. The German team from the small city of Böblingen, based near Joe's army deployment at Stuttgart, chose Joe and Banion to play for them. Playing for this team enabled Joe to play high-quality basketball with solid players in Europe who played a highly physical game. It also enabled him to travel to Switzerland, Italy, and France and feel comfortable with his presence in a far larger world than that open to most Americans with dark skin in "the land of the free and the home of the brave."

Finally, his European experience opened a world where skin color did not determine superiority and inferiority. Joe comments that in all his experience playing with White Europeans and before White spectators, not once did he hear the "N-word." It was only upon his return to the United States that he was once again subjected to racial taunts disparaging his skin color and was presumed inferior to those with a lighter skin tone.

Even in what Joe sometimes considers a "dark period" of his life, the lessons learned in Germany became the fundamentals he would teach other young people whose life circumstances he knew all too well: physical conditioning is important. Always place team performance above individual statistics. Never underestimate what can be achieved if you are willing to work hard. Everyone has a right to a bigger slice of the world in which to work and play—go for it!

THE RETURN HOME: PUTTING THE PIECES OF THE PUZZLE TOGETHER

Joe returned to civilian life at the end of 1972. The reunion of Joe and Bernice was a welcome one—nearly three years of separation had been difficult for them both. The long stretch of time apart from one another was not what they had expected before the draft and military service had taken over. Being together was what they had planned for all along.

Yet, each had adjustments to make. Michael was nearly three years old before Joe held him in his arms and looked into his eyes. Getting back to civilian employment and earning a living for his family was front and center in his mind. Upon returning from military service, Joe went to work for the Salem General Electric plant, which had held a spot for him during his deployment. Over the next few years, Joe completed a two-year degree in management and supervision at Virginia Western Community College. After a General Electric layoff, he secured a well-paying position at Mohawk Tire.

Bernice had been in charge of the home front during Joe's deployment, taking care of family matters and raising their sons. Though parenting would become a shared occupation, Bernice continued to be in charge of supporting their son's education. As a result, Michael was way ahead of his peers in reading—so much so that the principal at Lincoln Terrace Elementary School urged Bernice not to transfer him to another school because Michael's reading ability was important in the school's effort to qualify for a prestigious PLATO educational advancement program.

Before long, the family would have a new addition, James, who was born in 1974. As the children grew older, Bernice was the parent who had time to accompany them to the football games and practice sessions with the Inner City Athletic Association (ICAA). She wanted to make sure that her sons were treated well by local coaches and, frankly, not abused by leaders who could get so invested in winning that they forgot that the player they yelled at was still a child. Ironically, it was Bernice, not Joe, who first connected with volunteer coaches and their wives, held bake sales, and took money out of her own pocket to scrape enough together to pay for the necessary sports equipment and uniforms for the young Black players of their community.

Joe, Bernice, James, and Michael Gaither in the late 1970s. Photo by Laura Gaither, in front of her house.

While Joe was bringing in extremely good paychecks from Mohawk Tire, his work hours prevented him from joining Bernice and his sons at their ICAA evening football games and practice sessions. This was especially true when the company put him on the 3 p.m. to 11 p.m. shift. In addition to everything else she was handling, Joe had tasked Bernice with taking notes on what happened in team games and practices and reporting to him when he got home late at night.

Fortunately, an administrative job opened at the local post office. Though the job didn't promise a full 40 hours a week or that it would become permanent, Bernice remembers thinking, "Take the job, and I won't have to make these darn reports, and we can avoid divorce court." Joe applied.

He got his interview and was sent to compete in a required test with the other applicants. The test took place in a large room filled with applicants, of which he was the only man. Each applicant sat in front of a typewriter. Once again, it was Joe who got the job, thanks to the foresight of typing teacher Mrs. Judy Hoffler.

The chief metaphor for life is a picture puzzle. At every moment of our lives, we are presented with pieces to that puzzle. Sometimes it's obvious how those pieces fit together. Other times we have to look harder. Often, those pieces alone don't complete the puzzle. It is up to us to find or create the missing pieces, without which the picture ends up with holes and leaves us unsatisfied. We may have an idea of what the picture will look like when the last piece is put into place. Other times, when the last piece goes in, the picture may be so different that it surprises us with its unexpected beauty.

Joe was working on what that picture of his life was to be. Some of the pieces had been there before his military service. There was his mother, the part of the puzzle whose presence would always shape the larger picture of his life. There were the pieces of faith and church. There was his wife, the love of his life, who had been part of his picture since his youth. There were also new pieces in the puzzle, including his two sons and other pieces on the way. Yet there was a big piece he felt was missing: his mission in life.

COACHING, MENTORING, CHANGING LIVES

One day in the 1970s, a group of men from a Roanoke City neighborhood caught some kids breaking into a store. The men stopped the kids and asked them why they were resorting to robbery as a pastime. The youngsters explained that they had nothing else to do. What they wanted was to play ball, but they couldn't afford uniforms, and no one would sponsor them. The men, Rev. Robert Jeffrey, Nebraska Showalter, and Paul Moyer, then raised some donations for uniforms and organized the Inner City Athletic Association.

With more time on his hands due to his new, less demanding job, Joe became involved in the ICAA. Michael and James played on the ICAA sandlot football teams. Paul Moyer, the head of ICAA, asked Joe to be his assistant football coach in 1979. After a successful season, Paul suggested that Joe add basketball to the organization's offerings.

Soon, Joe was the head coach for two basketball teams. On Tuesdays and Thursdays, he coached a team of 11- and 12-year-olds, and on Wednesdays and Fridays, he coached 13- and 14-year-olds. Bernice remembers Joe's dedication. She says she could always tell how well his team had played a game just by how Joe put his key in the door.

Coaching revealed a talent that Joe was never aware of—the ability to instill in young men the values of confidence born of hard work, responsibility, courtesy, respect for others, sound judgment, and a knowledge of God's love and presence in their lives.

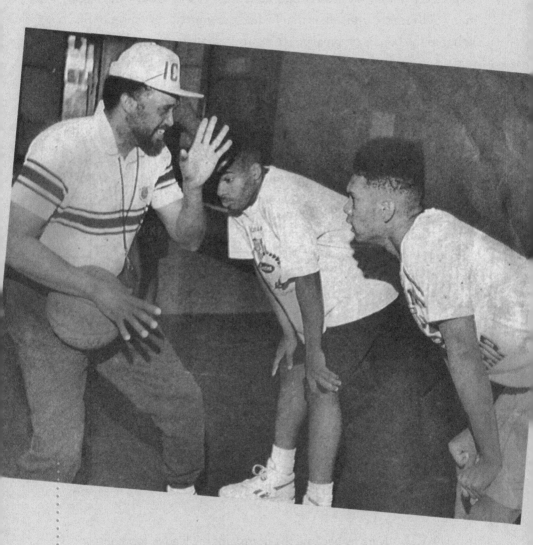

Joe coaches two young Hawks in the 1980s.
Photo by Eric Brady for The Roanoke Times.

One of Joe's neighbors in the Wilmont community asked why he coached the young people from Roanoke's poorest neighborhoods. He responded that he felt most comfortable with young people who faced many of the same difficulties that he had growing up: the absence of a father in the home; the presence of a strong mother who had to shoulder raising children alone, often by working two jobs; uncertain belief in themselves; and a lack of contact with an outside world of educational opportunity that could transform their lives.

Reflecting on those early days of coaching for ICAA, Joe reminisces:

> The one thing that truly attracted me to volunteering my time to work with youth in the Inner City was the one thing we had in common. Many of the young people that I coached were growing up in single-parent homes. I could identify with the void in a young man's life with only a mother trying to fill both the roles of parenting. The Inner City Athletic Association, led by Mr. Paul "Creedy" Moyer, introduced me to the coaching and mentoring that would truly give me a sense of fulfillment. I was also trying to learn to be a good parent myself to my two sons, James and Michael.
>
> Many of the kids were searching for a sense of purpose and camaraderie through the struggles they faced in their daily home lives. Creedy always emphasized the importance of strong discipline, maintaining their grades, and the power of prayer! We always began every practice with prayer and ended it in the Lord's Prayer. Each player was given an opportunity to lead that prayer. I can still hear the players asking in unison, "Can I be the preacher today?"

The ICAA Falcons became the dominant rec league football program in the Roanoke Valley, winning championships in every age group. The black and red Falcon uniform was a badge of honor, and the team became the talk of the Valley. Soon, under Joe's leadership, the ICAA basketball teams also began to dominate the field. He said, "This was the beginning of an awesome era of domination in the City, with

ICAA winning basketball championships in 1986 through 1991." The scores of league-winning basketball plaques from this period still hang in Joe's house testify to that achievement.

Roanoke ICAA team from the 1980s. They were state champions of the recreation league for 11- and 12-year-olds, with a 28-0 record. Photo by Bernice Gaither.

Bernice also stayed active with the ICAA during this time. Before girls were engaged in sandlot sports, they were recruited as cheerleaders. Uniforms for the young women were as important as the uniforms for players on the field. Bake sales, car washes, chicken dinners, and other fundraisers were created to offset the cost of the equipment. The organization had raised funds for the sweaters for the cheerleaders, but they could not afford the skirts. So Bernice, an excellent seamstress who had learned the skill from her mother, volunteered night after night to sew the skirts for the cheerleaders.

Coaching and mentoring young athletes were the missing pieces of Joe's life puzzle. All the other pieces instantly fit. He knew the young people he worked with better than they knew themselves. He knew the struggles of their families because he had experienced them as well. He knew the void they felt at the center of their lives because he felt the same void as a youngster. He knew their dreams because he also had them. He knew their frustrations because he had lived through them. He knew the difference a male role model can make in a young man's life.

And Joe Gaither knew how to win at basketball. Some of his wisdom came from his military experience. Until basic training, he had never experienced what it was to be in top physical condition and the impact of that conditioning on your level of competition. He now understood that the team in the best physical condition would often be the team that finishes with the best record. By the fourth quarter, the team in the best physical shape can jump higher and grab the decisive rebound, make a last-minute steal, fake out a defender, or outrun an opponent in a fast break. Joe's practice sessions were demanding workouts far beyond what other coaches expected. His players excelled because those drills gave them the stamina that made all the difference. Joe reminded his team, and they reminded each other, that "inspiration comes from perspiration."

Joe laughs when he talks about a later time when he coached basketball at a private school. An average drill began with a six-mile run, then fireman and bell weight drills up an incredibly steep incline, and another six-mile sprint before practice. When the players started to balk, a Lithuanian team member set the private school students straight. He had come to the U.S. to get a college athletic scholarship and a university degree. It was these workouts that would get both him and his teammates to that goal. "Shut up, do the workout, and be grateful," the foreign student advised them.

Further, in both the military and basketball, you are part of a team. The team performance, in the long run, outweighs individual performance. Joe put it simply, "The name on the front of the jersey, the team name, was always more important than the name on the back of the jersey, the player's name." What the team needs to win is more important than building individual player statistics. If three-point goals are needed in a game, the best three-point shooters are expected to be put on the court. If rebounds are needed, the best rebounders are called for. If speed is needed, then the fastest players get game time. If one scorer is having a bad day, it is the role of the rest of the team to make up the difference by playing beyond their past capabilities.

Finally, there is no substitute for respect. When addressed by a supervising officer or coach, only two responses are acceptable. No shrugs or head moments or gutturals like "uh-huh." Just two: "yes, sir," and "no, sir." There is also no substitute for respect for one another or the referee. Joe often reminded his players, "You have to anticipate bad calls! That is why you have to score additional points that will offset those referee errors." He never cursed or yelled at a player. He made sure he was never out of control and never got a technical foul called on him. "No grandstanding" is always the rule for coaches as well as players.

Make no mistake—Joe was about winning. At the same time, it was always more than that. It was about building young men of character whose score in the game of life was more important than that on a gym scoreboard. He once questioned another coach about his constant use of profanity in addressing his players. The man replied, "I signed on to win basketball games, not to be a social worker!" Joe let him know that he'd missed the point. He was there to build character in these young men that would continue for the rest of his players' lives and into the many arenas that life would take the young men.

Joe recalls the day Keith Hamilton showed up for practice with the Roanoke Hawks AAU team. Already a top football player at athletic powerhouse Lynchburg Heritage High School, Keith's physical presence was impressive at 6'7" and 265 pounds. Joe noticed him with no more fanfare than if he had been 5'2" and 120 pounds. Joe told the young man to take off his gold earrings and necklaces, put on his basketball shoes, and join the team. Keith, as if hit by lightning, did not move and stared at Joe in disbelief. One can only imagine what he was thinking: "Do you know who I am? Who in the hell do you think you are? I'm out of here!" Thirty seconds ticked by as the two looked at each other. Then, without a word from either party, Keith took off the gold, put on his shoes, and joined the team.

Later, Keith would tell his dad, "Coach Gaither doesn't put his hands on you, yell, or curse you. He just has a presence that is so powerful that it commands your respect." It was not Keith's size, strength, or athletic reputation that Joe was looking for. It was Keith's potential depth of character behind his pretension of importance. Keith joined the team because he saw, within a few seconds, that he had come to the right gym to train with the right coach.

More than two decades later, psychologist Angela Dawson would write about a character trait that determined which child would win the school spelling contest, which entering freshmen at the West Point or Annapolis academies would graduate in the top ten percent of their class, or which entrepreneur would be the most successful in their career. Her research discovered that—more than life experience, greater than the influence of IQ or any other factor—combined heightened levels of passion and perseverance made the difference in success rate. She termed that trait "grit."

Joe was already teaching his basketball players how to develop that level of power and perseverance, become grittier human beings, and achieve goals that they never thought were possible. He taught them that each workout, each scrimmage, and each game could be a growth experience. That "winners really win, not by bragging on their past achievements, but by daring to reach farther than their grasp." To look for greater challenges rather than relying on past accomplishments. That players win not with native talent but by developing a "will that can take them beyond their skill."

Off the court, Joe made sure his players focused on their performance in the classroom. Indeed, in many cases their athletic achievements could be the gateway to educational opportunities at a college or university if they completed high school with a good academic record. No matter their athletic achievements, they had to be coupled with good grades in the classroom.

Joe also showed his players the importance of service to others. All of his 25-year coaching career with the ICAA basketball program and the AAU Hawks was as a volunteer. His volunteerism extended beyond the basketball court to the players' homes. Other coaches did not visit their homes and help family members deal with problems of unemployment or a leaky roof. Even later, as a paid coach, Joe's salary barely covered expenses. His players knew that. It is not surprising that many of them ended up gladly spending their time coaching others.

Joe in the motor pool of the Roanoke post office. In 1993, he won the U.S. Postal Service of the Year Award for volunteering with the ICAA. Photo by Roger Hart for The Roanoke Times.

THE ICAA & TAP CONNECTION

During the late 1980s, Joe connected with the President and CEO of Total Action Against Poverty (TAP), Ted Edlich. As a Community Action Agency, TAP made it a point to work with low-income and minority organizations that were already striving to make improvements in their communities. Ted became interested in the ICAA because of the organization's efforts to strengthen a new generation of leadership in the community. In addition, Ted and his brother Dick had played little league baseball in Long Island, New York, and knew first-hand how transformative sports could be for youth.

Ted also liked that the ICAA was more than an athletic program—it also encouraged players to do well in school. It was the policy of ICAA to insist that their students maintain at least a C average in their studies. Team members were required to bring their report cards to practice. ICAA later coordinated with local afterschool programs like Straight Street and the West End Center, which helped students with their schoolwork if they fell behind in their studies. If there was a discipline problem in school, all the teacher had to do was give one of the ICAA coaches a call, and a visit to the school would correct the situation.

TAP offered a myriad of services for low-income families, including housing repair and weatherization, job training, Head Start preschool, a food bank, and more. The organization proved to be an invaluable resource for the ICAA and its players. When a single mother struggled to earn a living and provide decent and affordable housing for her family, Joe contacted Ted so that TAP could provide job training. When a family's roof needed repairs to keep water out when it rained, or the furnace died in the middle of winter and needed to be replaced, TAP stepped in to help. If TAP could not provide assistance, they would recruit other agencies to meet the need. Over the next decade, the calls for assistance to ICAA families grew, and the timely responses multiplied.

TAP's partnership with Roanoke City Council and the Roanoke city manager helped create goodwill in place of the bureaucratic inattention often experienced by poor neighborhoods. A simple call from the TAP CEO resulted in the city manager locating funds to erect night lighting for the ICAA athletic field in a neighborhood with unmet infrastructure needs.

The ICAA had incredible men and women who provided the coaching and mentoring. What they lacked was financial resources. Too much time was spent raising meager proceeds from the bake sales and hotdog roasts on which athletic equipment, team uniforms, and transportation depended. Ted used his connections to reach out to a group of White businessmen—including Heywood Fralin, Sen. Granger McFarlane, Mike Warner, Glen Combs, Steve Bowery, and Bittle Porterfield—who met with the coaches and agreed to join the ICAA board.

The support of businesspeople had a critical impact on the ICAA. The number of coaches, teams, and children served was increased. New sports like soccer were added to the list of offerings. It was truly a great partnership. The Black coaches and their wives knew the children and were trusted by their families. The White businessmen, who wanted to have a positive influence on the community, had the resources needed to cover the equipment, uniforms, and travel expenses that were otherwise out of reach for families who could not shoulder the cost.

THE ROANOKE HAWKS AND AAU BASKETBALL

With the ICAA teams dominating the league, it wasn't long before Joe issued his players a new challenge: "I know that you have worked hard and played great ball. You have beaten the best talent in your home area. But don't stop there. Why not see just how good you are against the best AAU basketball talent in the state and the nation?" The youngsters rose to the challenge, and the Roanoke Hawks AAU team was born.

The Hawks provided inner-city youth with three new opportunities. First, they were able to experience playing against the best talent from other areas. Second, they could expand their geographic horizons from the inner-city of Roanoke, Virginia, to major cities across the United States: Chicago, Los Angeles, Austin, Seattle, Miami, Memphis, and more. Joe did not want his players to turn down a college athletic scholarship because the distance of 140 miles from home seemed too overwhelming, as it had to him when he had been offered a scholarship to play for Bridgewater College. AAU participation could help his players feel at home in a bigger share of geography.

Lastly, the national AAU arena could increase player visibility among those who mattered for the young athletes' futures. Both state and national AAU championship tournaments were well-attended by college coaches from across the nation, searching for exceptional talent to strengthen their programs.

These coaches were increasingly drawn to the Hawks because Joe insisted that his athletes play with great intensity and always conduct themselves with the highest level of composure and dignity—behavior sought on college courts from coast to coast. Again and again, university basketball scouts and coaches complimented Joe and the Hawks for their conduct on and off the court.

It's important to note that while Joe was the Roanoke Hawks coach, as in all things, Bernice was right beside him. She made travel arrangements, took trips with the team, and frequently was called on to drive one of the vans. It was important for both of them that the AAU trips across the country were not just about basketball. The Gaither team insisted that the visit to each city be an educational experience. Bernice developed cultural itineraries everywhere they visited. When the Hawks visited Memphis, the team was taken to the pulpit from which Martin Luther King Jr. preached his famous "I've Been to the Mountaintop" sermon. They also went to the National Civil Rights Museum on the site of the Lorraine Motel, where an assassin took the American prophet and Nobel Peace Prize winner's life.

The other person that was right there with Joe was Associate Coach William Pannell. William had been one of the first coaches for ICAA. Joe served as an assistant coach to one of his football teams, and he was a constant as Joe's assistant ICAA basketball coach. William would continue to play that role for most of the AAU teams that Joe coached.

In some ways, working with the AAU players was more challenging because they came from different neighborhoods, schools, and localities. William and Joe often rode around in a pickup truck, making sure they got all the kids to practice on time and then safely home at the end of the day—all after working their full-time jobs that day.

William's "day job," which paid the mortgage and put food on his family's table, was with the Norfolk and Western Railway. Based in Roanoke, the railroad company built its own coal cars and served as a hub between the northeast, southeast, and west. Every day, long lines of empty coal cars passed through the Roanoke hub to West Virginia, the heart of U.S. coal mines. Within hours they returned fully loaded, many heading to marine ports in Virginia's Tidewater region.

Norfolk and Western was a source of reliable employment, good wages, and advancement opportunities for Black Roanokers. William was a laborer working in the East End and Shaffer's Crossing railway yards. Each year, he would note the dates for the upcoming national AAU tournament and request those days as part of his annual leave offered by the company. His supervisors were glad to approve his requests because they supported what he was doing for the community's youth. Sometimes they even threw in an extension, knowing that the tournament might be on the West Coast and require more time for travel.

Over the two decades in which the Roanoke Hawks played AAU basketball, they won 17 state titles. Joe and William's teams were also frequent contenders in the national AAU championships, placing second in Seattle, WA; third in Orlando, FL; fifth in Kingsport, TN; seventh in New Orleans, LA; and ninth in Baton Rouge, LA.

As word of the Hawks' state and national success spread, Joe gained an increasing reputation as the premier coach for athletes who wanted to study and train under the best in the business. Both Black and White athletes from Salem, Lynchburg, Martinsville, and other surrounding areas made the trek to play for Joe and the Hawks.

Joe enjoys telling the story of the time when the Hawks were invited to a basketball camp in Georgia that drew 16 teams from the southeast. The second day of the camp featured a dunk contest, which calls on a combination of the athleticism and acrobatic skills of its contestants, who seem to defy gravity as they soar above and around the basket, finally jamming the ball through the hoop. No one drew more laughs, ridicule, and surprise than Joe, who entered Philip Martin, a White kid from Buchanan, Virginia, as one of the Hawks' contestants. The laughter soon turned to applause as Philip soared higher and hung in the air longer than his competitors, winning the dunk contest. What Joe was aware of that no one else knew: Philip was the high jump champion for the Botetourt County high school track team.

Joe made good on his mission to help his players attain college

Coach Gaither after winning the
Mount Zion Invitational in Durham,
North Carolina, against Kevin
Durant's team.

scholarships, admissions, and four-year degrees, helping scores of his athletes achieve that goal. While he knew the AAU experience would help gain scout exposure for his players, he also realized that many of them needed an extra academic year to prepare themselves for the rigors of a university classroom and the pressures of being a college athlete. If an extra year could also help them develop their athletic skills in a highly competitive environment, so much the better. Joe often reached out to Virginia's Fork Union and Hargrave military academies on behalf of his players for that important preparation.

As a result, many of his players received scholarships to play their last two years of high school (their ordinary senior year plus an additional year) at these prestigious private military academies. A few of those players and the universities they played for as a result of these prep school experiences are Shannon Taylor (UVA), Boo Battle (UVA), Johnathan Mack (Northwestern), Juan Hankins (Wingate), Dwayne Priest (Eastern Michigan), and Jermaine Hardy (UVA).

Nothing appealed to Joe more than breaking stereotypes. Whether it was by taking a group of young men from poor, segregated Black neighborhoods to the semifinals and finals of national AAU play (and helping them earn a college scholarship along the way) or by forming an AAU team from a small section of southwest Virginia to defeat teams that drew talent from the entirety of Chicago or Los Angeles. Few things made the full-time postal employee/volunteer basketball coach happier.

WILLIAM FLEMING
JUNIOR VARSITY COACH

Since many players on the Hawks AAU team also played on the Patrick Henry High School varsity basketball team, Woody Deans, the Patrick Henry basketball coach, gave Joe a key to the school gym so that his other players could benefit from Joe's demanding Hawks workouts—which invariably helped the Patrick Henry team to win statewide tournaments.

However, when Patrick Henry High School decided to hire a junior varsity basketball coach, they were slow to consider Joe. Ironically, Patrick Henry's loss became the gain of their Roanoke City competitor, William Fleming High School. Alyce Szathmary, the outstanding William Fleming principal, wasted no time. She and her athletic director, the legendary "Killer" Miller, immediately recruited Joe to be the new JV coach. Joe held that position for the next decade. Beside him again was his right-hand man, assistant junior varsity coach William Pannell.

Led by this coaching team, the William Fleming JV boys' basketball team beat Patrick Henry for the Roanoke City basketball title ten years in a row, winning all 22 contests without a single loss!

Many consider Szathmary one of the most outstanding high school principals in Roanoke City over the last half-century. She created a community of staff, parents, and students who were listened to and pushed William Fleming to be a place where students thrived. About Joe, she said:

Few people had a greater impact on our students, the school, and the community. I have seen him take the toughest young man, angry at himself and the world, and turn him around into a totally different person, with hope for the future and a willingness to work hard. Joe's caring for a student rarely stopped at the end of the day. He would reach out to the boy's family and do whatever he could do make life better for them. Of course, he had an unmatchable winning record with our team. However, it was more than that. His incredibly positive presence impacted our entire school. There is no one I respect more than Joe Gaither, as a man, coach, and an educator!

Looking back on his days with the William Fleming team, Joe recalls starting the very first practice by putting up large signs around the gym which bore key words: CHARACTER, INTEGRITY, HONESTY, HARD WORK, and RESPECT. He began each the season not with basketball drills, but with creating a culture that developed character. Joe comments, "These values and behavioral traits were the mental and spiritual muscle on which our athleticism was built." His 22-0 record on the basketball court confirmed the wisdom of his strategy.

William Fleming junior varsity basketball team.
They were Blue Ridge District champions
in 1994-1995 with a 19-1 record.

ROANOKE CATHOLIC SCHOOL CELTICS

When Roanoke Catholic School was seeking a new basketball coach for the Celtics in 2004, local businessman Steve Bowery suggested that Headmaster Ray Correia consider the William Fleming JV coach, Joe Gaither, whose reputation for success had grown far and wide.

In their final meeting, after all matters of a contract had been discussed and agreed on, Ray asked Joe if he had any last-minute concerns. The headmaster was surprised when the prospective coach said, "I have one other major issue!" Ray undoubtedly expected that, as usual in staff negotiations, the concern was about money. He was visibly relieved when Joe said, "I want to be sure that I will be able to pray with my team on the court, before and after the game. That is something I could not do while working for a public school." Joe was hired.

The first thing that Joe did after being named the Celtics' head coach was reach out to Pat King, the middle school and JV coach at Roanoke Catholic. It wasn't long before the two realized a deep bond. Pat recalls:

> Joe had long believed in three-dimensional coaching, in developing the physical, emotional, and spiritual well-being of his players. At Roanoke Catholic, he worked with a diverse group of young men with backgrounds ranging from the rough inner-city to affluent suburbs to foreign exchange players. He hoped that a religious school like Roanoke Catholic would enable him to be even more open about the spiritual dimension of coaching.

The Roanoke Catholic basketball team prays after winning a state championship in VIS Division II. Photo by Fred Logan.

I admired Joe's emphasis on old-school basketball fundamentals, tough physical conditioning, and respect for authority. I knew he was in for a bit of a rough adjustment period at a place like Catholic, but I liked his no-nonsense approach. I admired his sincerity, and it didn't take us long to become friends.

Over time, Pat came to see that, in addition to being a gifted basketball coach, Joe intended to be a spiritual guide for his players and his colleagues. "I wasn't sure how that would work at first, considering this was a Catholic School and Joe was a committed Baptist, but I soon realized that wasn't going to be a problem. Joe's faith was so deep and sincere that no one had an issue with his openness about it."

Following the legendary coach Dick Wall—whose Celtics won three straight state titles from 2002-2004—was a challenge that only Joe would be up for. In his first year, the Celtics won the state title, winning 31 games out of a grueling 38-game schedule. That year, as one of 24 top high school basketball teams in the southeast, the Celtics were invited to compete in the Bull City Classic in Durham, North Carolina. They emerged as the 2005 Bull City Classic Champions in that hard-fought competition.

Roanoke Catholic basketball team that won back-to-back state championships in 2005 and 2006 in VIS Division II. Photo by Fred Logan.

That was also the year that Dr. Deneen Evans, the director of Multicultural Affairs at Roanoke College, secured a grant to bring Ken Carter, subject of the the movie *Coach Carter*, to Roanoke. The movie celebrated Coach Carter's closing the high school gym to all boys' basketball games until all members of his Richmond, California, team had improved their academic performances to ensure their college acceptance upon graduation. In addition to premiering the movie at Roanoke's historic Grandin Theater, Ken Carter made personal appearances at Roanoke City schools and Roanoke Catholic School where he shared his story to students, faculty, and parents.

Dr. Evans and her husband had elected to send their 6' 9" son, Brandon, to Roanoke Catholic School so he would have the advantages of a collage preparatory curriculum and training under Joe, considered by many to be the top secondary school athletic coach in the area. If there were ever two coaches cut from the same cloth, they were Joe Gaither and Ken Carter. Both emphasized the same values: top physical conditioning through hard work, the priority of building character through respect for others, accountability for one's action, willingness to sacrifice for the team, and the importance of educational achievement as the primary goal of being a student athlete.

In the 2005-06 season, the Celtics were state champions again after a 22-12 win-loss record. In the 2006-07 season, the Celtics came close to a repeat performance, but lost in the finals. Throughout Joe's career at Roanoke Catholic, the team almost always made the semifinals as one of the top four teams in their division. In 2008, Joe celebrated his 100th win with the Celtics after a mid-season game in Richlands, VA. All players from both teams signed the game ball, which was presented to Joe in front of the entire audience.

Game ball from the 100th win with the Roanoke Catholic Celtics in 2008. Detail from the cover photo by Greg Kiser Photography.

Local business and community leader Eddie Smith was at that game. A Methodist, he too had enrolled his son at Roanoke Catholic just so he could experience being coached by the best. He recalls:

> One of my fondest memories was seeing Coach Gaither achieve his 100th victory at Roanoke Catholic. My son was a freshman on that team. Unbeknownst to Coach Gaither, the team gathered prior to the game to sign a basketball signifying the 100th win. After signing the basketball, the team delivered a win that evening and then presented Coach Gaither with the autographed basketball. It was an incredibly meaningful moment. Coach Gaither had earned the love and respect of the players and they played their hearts out for him.

Aside from offering a first-rate basketball team, Roanoke Catholic was an excellent opportunity for Black students who needed educational settings with smaller classrooms than their public schools could offer, where respect for teachers was a requirement, where the majority of students expected to go on to college, and where social capital could be obtained by developing relationships with students and families who didn't come from economically and racially segregated neighborhoods. One such player was Kalleone Moret.

Like many inner-city teenagers, Kalleone sometimes found himself in trouble. He had even spent a little time in juvenile detention. Joe knew Kalleone from local basketball leagues and understood that he was a bright kid with a hard-working mom and an incarcerated father, and that he needed some extra guidance and opportunity.

Along with Pat, Joe helped Kalleone get into Roanoke Catholic for high school. Kalleone struggled with the new environment at first, but eventually made progress and was able to learn valuable skills. He stayed through his junior year, then transferred to Patrick Henry for his senior season.

Joe and Pat continued to mentor Kalleone and follow his basketball career at Patrick Henry. He played well at PH and received a scholarship offer to play basketball at Bluefield College. However, Kalleone didn't adapt well to college life, and left Bluefield early in his freshman year. Both Joe and Pat were concerned that he was at loose ends, but they stayed in touch and didn't forget about him.

The following summer, young Glenville State Assistant Basketball Coach Joe Mazzulla (now with the Boston Celtics) came to Roanoke to hold an open gym, looking for talent. Of course, because of Joe's long-standing reputation in the basketball world, Coach Mazzulla contacted Joe to see who might be interested in auditioning for an opportunity. Joe and Pat reached out to Kalleone and some other young men they were concerned about and brought them in for one last shot at college basketball.

Based on Joe and Pat's recommendation and what he saw at the open gym, Coach Mazzulla offered Kalleone a provisional scholarship to Glenville State. With constant support from both Joe and Pat, Kalleone made the best of this opportunity. Despite a severe knee injury, he played four years for Glenville State and graduated from their business school with honors. Today, Kalleone is a proud father and has a successful career in management logistics with a national transportation firm. He also mentors other young men.

Kalleone and Joe are still close. He explains:

> I owe so much to Coach Joe. I'm not sure where I'd be without him. He was tough on me, but he's been a great mentor and influence in my life. Coach Joe and Coach Pat stuck with me through thick and thin and never gave up on me even when I might have given up on myself. They helped make me the father and man I am today. I'll always be grateful.

Joe spent seven seasons as head coach at Roanoke Catholic. In all, he finished with an impressive record of 158 wins and 61 losses.

GAITHER JOINS STAPLES

In 2011, Joe was hired by the prestigious college prep Virginia Episcopal School in Lynchburg, Virginia as the assistant basketball coach under head coach Curtis Staples. The two knew each other extremely well—in fact, Joe had coached the former UVA basketball star since his participation as a youngster in the ICAA rec league and AAU Hawks. Years into their relationship, Joe also had a hand in Curtis's Christian confession of faith and baptism.

Curtis made it clear that "assistant coach" meant "associate coach," and that was how they worked together for the next eight years. The two would ultimately lead the team to an enviable record of 147 wins and 49 losses—an average of 18 wins and 6 losses per season—including three conference championships (2010-11, 2012-13, and 2013-14) and two state championships (2010-11 and 2015-16).

At the end of the 2010-11 winning season, Joe characteristically asked the team what they had learned from the season beyond the sport of basketball. Here are some of their answers:

COLIN PONDER (#42): "I learned what it means to make a commitment and follow through on it. About how to work and lead by example."

WILLIAM YU (#30): "You not only coached basketball, but also coached our life. You told us not to cut corners. You told us that what really matters is what we do when people can't see us.

You gave what can benefit our whole lives, no matter what field we are in."

FORD SPRINGER (#10): "I have heard too many pregame speeches in my life to count, but yours are the ones I know I will remember for the rest of my life. Each time you talk to us I feel like I came away from it as a better player, but more importantly a better person."[15]

---

15 VES Virginia Episcopal School 2010-2011 Varsity Boys Basket Ball Team
    Annual Report.

EDUCATIONAL AND CAREER IMPACT

Over his 25 years of coaching basketball with the Inner City Athletic Association teams, 11 years coaching the William Fleming junior varsity basketball squads, 17 years of coaching the Roanoke Hawks AAU teams, and serving as a coach for two top private schools in southwest Virginia, Joe has had a pivotal impact on the lives of up to 2,000 young athletes.

While we don't have the ability to document Joe's full impact, the following is a list of 89 of his athletes who were able to play at the collegiate level with the help of his training and guidance over his four-decade coaching career:

Anderson University: Tre Fields
Benedict College: Chris Black
Bluefield State College: Brian Dockery
Bryan University: Taylor McCue
Canisius College: Rokas Gricius
Coastal Carolina University: Brent Jenkins, Reginald Reynolds
Duke University: Chris Combs
East Carolina University: Caleb White
East Tennessee State University: Jason Niblett
Eastern Michigan University: Dwayne Priest
Elizabeth City State University: Derrick Hines, William Fitzgerald
Ferrum College: Eugene Cook, Mark Terry, Maurice Preston

George Mason University: Anthony Swann

Georgetown University: Dante Harris

Glenville State University: Kaleon Moret

Hampden-Sydney College: Marcus Caldwell, Tony Joyce,
    Turner King, Russell Turner

Hampton University: Philip Lacey

Indiana University of Pennsylvania: Jamare Crump

James Madison University: Bosco Williams, Robert Carson

Johnson C. Smith University: James Otey

Lees-McRae College: David Keaton

Long Island University: Aremus Adomitius

Longwood University: Brandon Evans, Isaac Belton,
    Landen Martin

McNeese State University: Bryan Price

New Mexico Highlands University: Mindaugus Marchevisius

Norfolk State University: Mark Ward, Mondre Burnette

North Carolina State University: Rodney Redd, Ronald Murphy

Northeastern University: Johnathan Mack

Ohio University: Ernie Hodge

Old Dominion University: Odell Hodge

Princeton University: Aaron Young

Radford University: Doug Day, Philip Martin, Raymond Arrignton

Seattle University: Delanta Jones

Tusculum University: Cory Poindexter

University of Cincinnati: Kenny Belton

University of Delaware: Greg Smith, Skyy Johnson

University of Kentucky: Sasha Jones

University of Missouri–St. Louis: Irmantus Cristus

University of New Hampshire: Chris Kay

University of North Carolina: George Lynch

University of North Carolina Asheville: Alphonso Ward

University of North Carolina Wilmington: Mark Byington

University of Pittsburgh: Justice Kithcart, Keith Hamilton

University of Rhode Island: Ifeanyi Onyekaba

University of Richmond: Curtis Blair, Gordon Winn

University of South Carolina: Jamie Price

University of Virginia: Curtis Staples, Dennis Haley, Devon Battle, Jermaine Hardy, Shannon Taylor

Virginia Military Institute: Craig McCargo, Eric Walker, Jon Baker, Matt Matheny, Perey Covington

Virginia State University: Michael Willis, Orlando Walker, Richard Wilson, Mark Grogan

Virginia Tech: Bernard Basham, Brandon Dillard, Pedro Edison, Jeff King, Jerome Preston, Michael Holland

Virginia Union University: Chris King

Wake Forest University: Philip Haynes

Weatherford College: Deangelo Robinson

Wingate University: Juan Hankins

Winston-Salem State University: Ronald Hubbard

Winthrop University: Philip Kaus

Many on the list are well-known from their subsequent athletic achievements, like Doug Day, Curtis Staples, Curtis Blair, George Lynch, Mark Byington, Russell Turner, and Keith Hamilton. These achievements are noted not to separate them out from the rest, but to indicate the high caliber of athleticism that Joe was able to engender in his players.

DOUG DAY was an outstanding shooting guard for Virginia's Radford University for four years beginning in the 1989-90 season. He led the NCAA in all-time three-point shots, with a total of 401 at graduation. He also led the Highlanders to their first Big South Conference men's basketball regular season championship, and their two consecutive 20-win seasons. In all four of his college seasons, he was named to the Big South All-Conference Team. Doug was inducted into the Radford University Hall of Fame in 1998 and the Big South Conference Hall of Fame in 2005.

CURTIS STAPLES was a University of Virginia basketball star, who is best known for taking the NCAA three-point career title from Doug Day, and holding the record at 413 until it was beaten by J.J. Redick of Duke. The university retired Curtis's jersey (#5) on November 12, 2006, during halftime of Virginia's first game in its new John Paul Jones Arena. Curtis ranks ninth on Virginia's career scoring list with 1,757 points. After playing several seasons of professional basketball overseas, Curtis became the head basketball coach at Virginia Episcopal School. He continues to coach at Lakeway Christian Academy in White Pines, Tennessee.

CURTIS BLAIR began his college career as a point guard for the University of Richmond Spiders. He was honored as the Colonial Athletic Association Men's Basketball Player of the Year in the 1991-92 season, and was a two-time First Team All-CAA selection and three-time CAA All-Tournament Team selection. In addition, he played for the Houston Rockets and overseas in Turkey. He is now an NBA referee.

GEORGE DEWITT LYNCH III still holds the University of North Carolina basketball record for most career steals. After leading UNC to a NCAA title in 1993, he was a first-round draft pick by the Los Angeles Lakers. George later played for the Vancouver Grizzlies, Philadelphia 76ers, and New Orleans Hornets. Following his playing years, he held coaching positions with Southern Methodist University and Clark Atlanta University. Finally, he is the co-founder of the nonprofit organization HBCU Heroes in Atlanta, Georgia.

MARK BYINGTON was a three-year starter for the UNC Wilmington team. There, he received two CAA All-Academic selections, as well as Second Team All-CAA and CAA All-Defensive Team honors. He then spent seven years as an assistant coach with the College of Charleston before becoming head coach at Georgia Southern University for seven outstanding seasons. Mark is now the head coach for James Madison University and was named the 2020-21

CAA Coach of the Year.

RUSSELL TURNER attended Hampden-Sydney College, where he was named First Team All-ODAC for four consecutive years and a two-time All-American. Russell finished his college career as Hampden-Sydney's all-time leading scorer with a total of 2,272 points. After serving as assistant coach for Hampden-Sydney, Wake Forest University, Stanford University, and the NBA's Golden State Warriors, he became the head coach at University of California, Irvine. He has since been named Big West Coach of the Year four times and become the winningest coach in UCI history.

KEITH LAMARR HAMILTON played football at the University of Pittsburgh. He was selected in the 1992 NFL Draft by the New York Giants as a defensive tackle. He played with the Giants for 12 seasons and recorded 63 sacks, placing him fourth on the team's career sacks list. Known as "Hammer," Keith was named a Pro Bowl alternate in 2000, when he recorded ten sacks and played for the Giants in the 35th Super Bowl.

Keith Hamilton is not the only one on this list who ended up with a college scholarship for football rather than basketball. The nine others who would do so include: Bernard Basham (VT), Jerome Preston (VT), Rodney Redd (NC State), Shanon Taylor (UVA), Chris Combs, (Duke), Brandon Dillard (VT), Jeff King (VT), Johnathan Mack (Northeastern), and Eric Walker (VMI).

Joe explains the seeming contradiction that some of his players ended up playing college football rather than basketball with the following realities:

> First, all of these athletes played both football and basketball in high school. Second, each year there are more football college scholarships awarded than basketball scholarships. Third, fans forget that before the three-point shot opened up the game of basketball, most of the offensive play was right under the basket. The team with the biggest and strongest players

dominated the game by physically overcoming the opposition with their size and agility. It was as tough a game under the basket as it was in the frontline of a football game.

No one knew his players better than Joe. Of the 85 players listed above, 26 had played basketball for Joe in the ICAA rec league. He had known many since they were seven or eight years old. He was not only their coach, but their mentor, and in many cases a father figure. He was responsible for their performance on and off the court. He was often their academic counselor, responsible for helping them to strengthen their academic skill set and, when necessary, arranging for enrollment in top private college preparatory institutions. However, what most people don't know was that Joe was also his players' unpaid agent, who facilitated contact between the athletes and universities.

Reporting on a 1995 Kingsport, TN, basketball tournament for the Bristol Courier, sports journalist Allen Gregory wrote, "Joe Gaither doesn't wear a business suit or carry a cellular phone, but he is a power broker! "[16] It was Joe who built relationships with the college basketball scouts and athletic directors of more than 50 institutions of higher learning across the United States. To this day, he still carries many of their personal telephone numbers.

There were times that college coaches didn't take his advice but later wished that they had. Joe recalls making a call to University of Virginia basketball coach Jeff Jones, telling him that he ought to take a good look at Curtis Blair, one of the Hawks' top AAU ball players. Jones agreed to give Curtis a tryout, but ultimately decided that he wasn't fast enough for the team. It wasn't long before the University of Richmond recruited Curtis. After the first game that season between UVA and Richmond, Jones called Joe and told him that he should have taken Joe's advice—Curtis had destroyed the Cavaliers. Gaither smiled and said, "I tried to tell you."

---

16 Gregory, Allen. "Gaither Grooms Future Stars with Roanoke Hawks." Bristol Herald Courier, June 2, 1995.

IN THEIR OWN WORDS

Perhaps Joe's impact on the lives of his players is best described in the words of the players themselves. Below are the reflections of seven men on their time spent with Coach Joe.

SHANNON TAYLOR

Many people know me as the football coach for Northcross Schools in Roanoke, Virginia. I am 47 and Coach Joe has been an important part of my life for the last 37 years.

I grew up in the Landsdowne public housing projects where life is tough, drug transactions were frequent, stabbings occurred, and prostitution took place in the open. When I was ten years old my friend, Kenny Booker, and I wanted to try out for the Inner City Athletic Association sports teams.

ICAA pretty much dominated the football and basketball recreation leagues for decades when I was a kid. A big problem was that neither of us had transportation. Word got to Coach Joe, and he agreed to pick us up on his way down Salem Turnpike from his house in Wilmont Farms to the practice field, and to get us home after practice. Coach penciled me in as quarterback, taught me how to run a no-huddle offense, and I played football quarterback for the next few years. From our first meeting I realized that he was the strong male role model I needed in my life.

Joe Gaither was a big-time athlete, playing both basketball and football at G.W. Carver. He took me to his home in those early years and showed me pictures of his high school years. Even at Andrew Lewis High School, there are pictures of his senior year.

I played quarterback for Inner City Athletic football for four years. When I became a seventh grader in junior high school, he persuaded me to try out for the junior high football team. I became the seventh-grade backup quarterback to a ninth grader who was really good at that position.

When I graduated to the eighth grade, the school system abandoned organized athletic teams in middle schools. My only option was to play high school football as an eighth grader. Now that was scary! It was because Coach Joe had confidence in me, and I knew all the older guys from our association with Inner City Athletics, that I ended up playing both football and basketball at Patrick Henry High School. During the summers, I played AAU basketball with the Roanoke Hawks. You can't underestimate how much our experience under the coaching talents of Joe Gaither contributed to those teams in 1988 and 1982 who won state championships for Patrick Henry High School.

Although basketball became my first love, football was the sport where I would experience my greatest success. At 6'4" and 199 pounds, I was the ideal size for a quarterback but too short for basketball. My experience in running with the Inner City Athletic Association track team increased my speed, which together with arm strength and quickness, was ideal for quarterbacks. In my high school sophomore year as a starting quarterback, I was recognized by the media as a Pre-Season All American. I also had a great junior year playing football at Patrick Henry.

After that year, the number of college and boarding school scholarship offers just exploded. While I received offers for college basketball athletic scholarships from Auburn, Virginia Tech, and Wofford College, the offers from colleges and universities for football were off the charts, just ridiculous. I had offers coming from top schools in Florida, California, Virginia, and all over the country.

At the same time, I was experiencing academic problems that I needed to address. My GPA was very strong, but the SAT scores required by the institutions were too low for acceptance. Coach Joe suggested that I consider doing a prep school year at Fork Union Military Academy instead of Patrick Henry. There I would get the academic support that was not available in a local public high school.

So prior to my senior year, Coach Joe drove me to Fork Union

Military Academy in his baby blue station wagon to introduce me to the school. On the drive home that night, the car fishtailed on an icy bridge. Joe got the vehicle under control, but the situation unnerved me. Coach, a man of faith, pulled the car off the road and offered prayer. I got home all right, but the experience soured me on the idea of a senior year at Fork Union.

Frankly, I was uncertain about a lot of things. People in Salem and friends at William Fleming wanted me to play for their schools. I appealed to the City of Roanoke to allow me to attend Fleming but was denied by the school board. Coach Joe was by my side as I looked at my options and as I made my own decisions. I ended up playing my senior year at Patrick Henry, and had a great season topped by beating William Fleming High School in both games that year.

My father passed away when I was 15. My mom was a single mom. It was Coach Gaither who helped me navigate those years. When it became clear that my athletic future lay in football, it was Coach Gaither who contacted businessman Heywood Fralin and got us tickets to UVA football games. He introduced me to UVA defensive coach Danny Wilmer and arranged for me to go to the UVA football camp. Coach Joe further arranged for me to attend Fork Union Military School after my senior year at Patrick Henry High School to help me raise my SAT scores to meet UVA requirements. He helped find money to help our family in hard times. He was the one who drove me to the University of Virginia for my "redshirt" freshman year where I attended practices with the football team and had access to training facilities, but did not play games, giving me time to focus on academics.

I had a good year on the football field as a starter among the three linebackers. However, I failed to meet expectations in the classroom and was ruled ineligible to play in my junior year. Without the intervention of Coach Joe, that decision would have spelled the end of my college experience at UVA. Coach appealed to the dean of students to give me another chance. He put his reputation on the line, arguing I would meet my academic expectations at the university and make a significant contribution to the football program in my senior year if allowed to continue at UVA. Joe argued that sending me home might well be a death sentence or expulsion from a future of promise.

The dean rescinded the university decision. During my junior year I regained my academic standing as I applied myself in the classroom. At the end of five years, I graduated from the university with a major in anthropology and a minor in psychology. During my senior year I had a strong performance on the gridiron, leading the defense with 99 tackles, 15 tackles with a loss, and 6 quarterback sacks. Upon graduation I enjoyed a professional football career of a combined five and a half years with the San Diego Chargers, the Baltimore Ravens, and the Jacksonville Jaguars.

There is no question of the impact of Coach Joe Gaither on my life. He has been the father figure who made the continued difference in my life and family. When I was at Fork Union, my daughter was born. I am pleased that she is a college graduate of Wake Forrest University where she was also a member of the women's basketball program.

JERMAINE HARDY

I was a boy from the "projects." We lived in Lincoln Terrace public housing. I first met Coach Joe when I was 10 years old. I played ICAA football and basketball under Paul "Creedy" Moyer, Joe Gaither, and William Pannell until I was 13.

I attended William Fleming High School. Because of my prior training under ICAA, I was drafted to play on the Fleming varsity basketball team when others my age played for the junior varsity led by Coach Gaither.

Like so many of us coming through the projects, there was not much encouragement for academics. I thought C's were good enough. Coach "Killer" Miller knew that I aspired to one day play professional sports, hopefully the NFL. Coach Miller helped me create a blueprint for achieving my dreams. The plan meant that I would have to get a scholarship to play for a top school like the University of Virginia.

That meant that I would have to improve my grade point average and SAT scores. That was not going to happen without a more supportive environment in which I could develop the discipline to work as hard on my academics as I was on my athletics. From prior experience with other students, Coach Miller suggested that I transfer to Hargrave Military Academy for my senior year of high school. With his help I was able to get a scholarship, but that was a long way from a free ride. I would have to raise thousands of dollars to pay the difference in order to make the Hargrave experience a reality.

I had stayed in touch with Coach Gaither throughout my William Fleming years. I reached out to him, seeking his advice on how to proceed. Coach Joe agreed with Coach Miller and could see that I was serious in my desire to improve my academic standing. He contacted his network of donors and supporters in the business community and quickly raised the money necessary for me to attend Hargrave Military Academy.

I made good on my end of the deal. I worked hard, and by the end of the year at Hargrave Military Academy I had so improved my grade point average and SAT scores that I received a football scholarship to the University of Virginia. After graduation I went on to have a career in the NFL in the U.S. and Europe.

Everything followed from me getting into Hargrave. I'm forever grateful to Coach Joe and the Inner City Athletic Association for their help.

Today I am head coach of the Virginia Warriors Elite boys' basketball team in Roanoke, Virginia. We have won back-to-back National Travel Basketball Association championships in 2020 and 2021.

GEORGE LYNCH

When I was in the fifth grade, I had my first exposure to Coach Joe Gaither. It was not a good one. My friends and I decided to walk two miles from our neighborhood to Addison High School to try out for the Inner City Athletic Association football team. Joe Gaither was one of the coaches holding tryouts. The tryouts consisted of tough physical drills outside on a hot sunny day. The toughest exercise was that we had to do a bear walk the length of the field on the pads of our hands and feet carrying another person on our backs. After that exercise, we were worn out and still had two miles to walk to get back to our homes. All of us decided that day never to play with ICAA, especially if Joe Gaither was the coach. Instead, we signed up with the Optimist Club recreation football team. When it came time to play Coach Gaither's ICAA team, they destroyed our Optimist Club team. They were in much better shape, physically stronger, and much faster.

What we didn't realize at the time was that Coach Gaither was saving kids' lives by helping them define themselves at a deeper level through these tough drills. We define ourselves by the amount of effort, the hard work, we put in to be competitive and achieve what we want to get out of life.

I was fortunate to connect with Joe when I started playing basketball at Patrick Henry. We had a great group of talented basketball players coming through Roanoke Valley high schools at that time. Curtis Blair, Russell Turner, and Jason Niblett were among them. Many of these athletes had played basketball for Coach Gaither through the ICAA and national AAU competition with the Roanoke Hawks. Patrick Henry coach Woody Deans allowed the Roanoke Hawks to use the Patrick Henry High School gym. I joined the Hawks in the team that competed in the 15 & Under AAU tournament in Orlando, Florida (third place) and the 16 & Under AAU tournament in Arkansas (ninth place).

Coach Gaither believed in hard work and accountability. He expected discipline from those on the team, but he didn't overdo the discipline. He was not tough to be tough. He found ways to convince us that if we wanted to be successful, these were the things we had to do. We were guys who had a vision. He was our support system to achieve that vision.

Through AAU he gave us the opportunity to travel and see things outside Roanoke and connect with a larger world of talent and experience. He found ways to get older more experienced players to come in and play against us and raise our level of competition. He found ways to help all of us work together and pull in the same direction. He just seemed to say the right things at the right time. He knew what buttons to push. He knew that all of us had a sense of pride and wanted to represent the Roanoke Valley by being the best. He figured out ways to build on that pride and play off it.

We learned how to put up with obstacles. Back then, the Patrick Henry gym was one of the best facilities in the Roanoke Valley. However, it had no air conditioning. Summer practice in a hot gym where the only reprieve from the heat was opening small doors to the outside and getting a slight breeze was tough. I remember playing in Little Rock Arkansas during the summer. You were already sweating when you got out of bed in the morning. Then we had to walk to the gym in 90-degree heat.

We also had to deal with each other. Without the diversion of Facebook and Instagram, we had to handle our feelings, express ourselves, build relationships, and work as a team. Those were good times in which, by necessity, we built incredible relationships.

Coach Gaither had a sense of humor. In another life, he might have been a comedian. You remember those guys with their "momma" jokes. We were about to play a tough team in Oklahoma. I don't know if Coach Joe thought we were lagging in energy, but he called us together before game time. He looked at all of us and said, "Man, I was walking past the Oklahoma team and they were talking trash about you guys. Saying that you were pushovers and wondered how you even got to the tournament. Then they started talking about your mommas. I mean they were trash talking. How does that make you feel? You gonna let them get away with talking about your mommas?" No cuss words, but he found a way of motivating us by putting us in touch with another shot of adrenalin through the image of our competitors trash talking our mothers.

Those of us who played for the Hawks during summers were the core of the Patrick Henry High School basketball team that won the state championship. PH coach Woody Deans should get a great deal of credit for his coaching and our success. Most folks don't realize how much of that credit must also be shared with Joe Gaither and the three high school summers with the Roanoke Hawks.

One of the things I appreciate most is the quality of selflessness that has been part of the characters of all the coaches I have had. That includes those at every level including Dean Smith at the University of North Carolina and my professional career with the NBA. All of them have been selfless people.

Look at Joe Gaither. He had his own family, a wife and two sons. I suspect he has spent as much or more time with players he has coached than with his own family. Being with people like that has helped to shape me and those I have played with.

I am glad that we won the state championship in my junior year of high school. All of us had to sacrifice something to make that happen. None of us played with the goal of scoring the most points. We all sacrificed a part of our game to benefit the entire team. I have been fortunate to be with coaches who knew they had talented players but helped us to put the team above our need for individual recognition. It was the sacrifice that Joe and the other coaches made in putting our lives first that has made us into the people we are today with the values we can be proud of.

The first lesson I learned from Joe Gaither was that if you want to achieve your dreams in life you have to put in the hard work. The goals and achievements that I have had in life, I could not have achieved had I not learned the lesson that I had to put in the hard work. Hard work and willingness to sacrifice for the team's success are core pieces of producing winners in basketball and every other human endeavor.

EUGENE COOK

I was four years old when I met Coach Joe. My mom sent me out to the field where Joe was coaching ICAA football. Her plan was to leave me there, because she knew that the adults would look out for me. It was one of the few places outside my home where a kid was safe.

Mom was told that I was too young for the team and too young to be left alone. I started to cry. Coach Joe said he would make an exception. I started playing organized football at the age of four for Joe Gaither. When I was 13, I played AAU basketball for the Roanoke Hawks in the 13 & Under class. Our team would finish fourth in the nation in the tournament that was held in New Orleans. I played varsity football for Patrick Henry High School with fellow student Shannon Taylor. With the help of a football scholarship, I continued the sport at Ferrum College, graduating with a four-year B.A. degree.

Like so many youngsters in the Roanoke Valley of Virginia, Joe Gaither was part of my life before I was in the first grade. He had no interest in our being second-best athletes or second-best persons. He inspired us to work hard in what we did on the field or in the classroom. That meant both to be the best and to be respectful of others. He inspired a strong sense of pride in us, born out of hard work and using every experience to improve our performance. Often, he would make up a nickname that reminded us of an accomplishment. He said he could always tell when I made a tackle because I hit them so hard that their eyes would water. So he called me "Bluesey" for their watery eyes.

When you talked to others who have come through Joe's coaching and become coaches themselves, it is crazy that you hear them repeating the same words, thoughts, and phrases that you learned under Coach Joe when you were just a kid. "No half efforts. You got to be a dog, which means you got to be the baddest thing on the court!" "You have to have the same passion that Mohammed Ali had when he started boxing lessons as a kid after someone stole his brand-new bike." He'd challenge us in practice. "Can you give me one more push up? One more forty-yard sprint? One more tackle at a dummy?" He drove up our expectations for ourselves. "No touchdowns, no new first downs for the other side."

At the same time, Joe Gaither was a clean-cut guy. He told us that when we were out in society to respect others. It was "yes, sir" and "no, sir." He never cussed. He programmed us not only to be good athletes but good citizens, to handle ourselves with dignity, and to be accountable for our actions. When you were playing for his ICAA team and your school grades came out, you were expected to bring your report cards to the very next practice to demonstrate your accountability in the classroom. If a player had a need for shoes, Joe would see that he got the shoes. If you needed a reference for an activity or a job, you could count on him taking the time to get you that reference or to make a call on your behalf. On your part you wanted to be the person that lived up to deserving getting a reference from Joe Gaither.

Currently, I am head coach for the Patrick Henry High School girls' varsity basketball team. I have coached recreation league football and basketball. My college degree is in social work. I have coached teams that my son and daughter played for. I also run a program for mentally challenged adults, teaching them living skills. I try to incorporate what I have learned from Joe Gaither in helping others be their best.

CURTIS BLAIR

I played basketball for Joe Gaither for two years on the ICAA team before joining the Roanoke Hawks AAU team. Before my first meeting with Coach Gaither, I had heard many positive things about his basketball program and knew that he was a football coach as well. The word was that he was a tough and demanding coach. Many of his players came from tough circumstances. He emphasized discipline and being accountable for one's behavior, decisions, and actions.

I remember Coach Gaither getting his teams to sit down for 45 minutes or longer before we practiced and talk seriously about the importance of schoolwork and what it was going to take for us to succeed in life in the classroom and on the court. He explained how tough it was going to be to perform at the highest levels in all areas of life. He emphasized the importance of being mentally prepared for the challenge and learning to play for the team rather than ourselves. He stressed the importance of being good citizens as well as good athletes. He emphasized that success requires hard work. The path forward was in setting high goals and then the hard work to developing the mental and physical development to achieve them. He stressed the importance of listening to the coaches. Later he would introduce us to players who were older, whom he had trained. Scrimmaging with them challenged us to work harder and gain confidence in what we were learning. Later we would meet younger athletes with whom he was working and help them stretch their expectations of what they might achieve.

Joe Gaither ran hard practices, driving his players to push themselves harder than any other coach. They were intense, physically demanding, and unrelenting. When I was accepted at the University of Richmond, I met another coach who ran extremely tough and demanding workouts. I told Coach Joe that I was very grateful for my experience with his workouts. It was because of them that I was able to take the Spider coach's workouts in stride.

When I've coached basketball, I have continued what I have learned from Coach Gaither, especially discipline and accountability. Young people respond to those values as long as they know that you also care about them personally, aside from their performance on the court. A sense of playfulness is also important to soften the impact when we all make mistakes no matter how hard we try. This was the foundation that I learned from Joe Gaither. Others have built on that foundation. However, nothing replaces that foundation.

RUSSELL TURNER

During my early years, I played basketball with the Heights Club in Roanoke City. We had some of the best teams in the league alongside the dominant ICAA. Over time I got to know players on ICAA and their coaches. At Patrick Henry High School, I found myself on the same basketball team with some of their very best players, Curtis Blair and George Lynch. During the high school summer seasons, I played AAU basketball with the Roanoke Hawks under Coach Joe Gaither.

AAU with the Hawks gave me an opportunity to play with the very best players from the City of Roanoke and surrounding high schools. I liked the tough and demanding workouts and opportunities to play against older players who once played for the Hawks and were now playing in colleges around the country whom Coach purposefully arranged for us to play. These experiences toughened our wills and a sharpened our skills.

Coach Gaither's demanding workouts helped me realize the payoffs that hard work brings as we took on teams whose skills and experience were every bit as great as ours, and in some cases greater.

The thing I remember best from those days with Coach Gaither was his belief that no goal was outside our reach. I remember him looking us dead in the eyes and telling us that we had the capacity, drive, and ability to be the top AAU team for our age group in the nation.

The AAU finals brought the top AAU basketball players in the nation. No matter, we had the ability, the physical stamina, and the level of teamwork that would put us on top. Frankly, though I didn't say anything to challenge his estimate, I wondered if this was possible. Yet as we worked to meet this challenge and kept winning, I found myself acting on this belief. We were the best. We began to outplay our previous play, and his belief in that future became our belief, my belief.

Yes, Coach Gaither drove us to be physically stronger than our opponent. Yes, he kept finding competition that drove us to be better. But more than anything, he helped us believe as a team and as individuals that we had the capacity to be the best, the very best in the nation. That was the year that we, a group of athletes formed from a 60-mile radius from the City of Roanoke in the middle of Virginia, came in second the nation. We were in the circle of champions.

We were in a hotel, waiting to go to the court for that last game. He looked at us and said, "This is the most talented squad I have ever coached. Any one of you could someday have a career in professional sports." We went to the last game believing and playing as if that were true. And you know what? Six of us went on to have careers in the NBA or NFL as players, coaches, or referees.

Joe Gaither could make you believe that outstanding achievement, that being the best, is as likely as taking your next breath. He had the gift of true leadership. Looking back on those moments reminds me that, because of Coach, I had developed an almost irrational confidence that I could be on a team of winning players in the greatest of contests. That is the gift I have tried to pass on to my former players at the Golden State Warriors and my present teams at the University of California Irvine.

TONY JOYCE

I met Coach Joe Gaither when was nine years old. I played ICAA football under Coach Paul Moyer and Assistant Coach Gaither. These were men of faith, but I have to laugh when I think of how men of love could come up with some of the brutal exercises of physical conditioning that they required for those who played for their teams. Let me tell you it was tough love, with an accent on the "tough." The fact was that these coaches were pushing us to be the best we could be.

I was on one of the early AAU teams coached by Joe Gaither. I remember walking into a massive gym for a national AAU tournament in Indianapolis. A team which drew players from the entire metropolis of Los Angeles was warming up. They were incredibly slick, strong, and fast, more like high school players than 13-year-olds. They exuded the confidence of winners.

Coach Joe could tell from our body language that his team was getting intimidated by the bigger and stronger players from Los Angeles as they warmed up. He pulled us aside and explained that the LA team was made up of players just like ourselves and we had beaten teams better than the one we saw practicing on the floor. He assured us that this team of young Hawks could beat that team and anybody else if we believed in ourselves and acted with confidence in the players he had helped us to be. He literally convinced us that we were the best. And that day the Roanoke Hawks beat that team from the metropolis of Los Angeles!

Of course, Joe wanted us to be competitive. But he wanted more from his players. He wanted us to compete with grace and dignity. Why? Because the world does not expect grace and dignity from young

Black men. He always reminds us that the way we conducted ourselves reflected on us, on him, on our parents, and our community.

One more thing: Joe was one of the main people in my life who made me feel like I needed to pay it forward, to coach and mentor young people myself. Nevertheless, it was not until I coached and mentored young men myself that I realized how much time and energy it takes to be a volunteer coach; to mentor young people with their various challenges; to ferry kids to practice and home after practice; to raise money to pay for travel and registration fees.

I received a scholarship to Roanoke Catholic School on a recommendation from Coach Gather. I also played football and basketball at Hampden-Sydney College. Subsequently, I was an assistant coach to Joe when Roanoke Catholic School won the Virginia Independent Schools State Championship in 2005 and 2006. Currently, I am the operations manager at Allstate and am a mentor with the 100 Black Men of Greater Charlotte.

DEACON GAITHER

From their earliest years, faith has been a part of Joe and Bernice's lives. The strong mothers of each one of them were both active church women and insisted that their children were grounded in the gospel and culture of the Black Christian church.

Even after they married, Bernice and Joe continued to attend different churches. That was, until Bernice heard a sermon with the message: "The family that prays together stays together." It was then that she decided to join Shiloh Baptist Church, which Joe had attended since childhood.

For many years, Joe was an occupant of the church's last seat nearest the door. Bernice said that Joe would beat her home, open a Miller Light, and have the television already tuned to pregame shows before she walked in the door. She remembers saying, "Well, that sermon didn't last long, did it?"

Joe explains it this way: "I was in the church, but the church wasn't in me. I know now God had been working in my life all along, but I did not yet have a personal relationship with the Lord. I knew about God, but I didn't know God."

Things changed when Adrian Dowell became Shiloh Baptist's pastor. The new pastor ministered to the hearts and minds of his congregation, sharing the profound teachings of the scriptures. He concentrated on the teachings of the church and their application in the real world for his parishioners.

When he lived and worked in Bluefield, West Virginia, Pastor

Dowell had learned of Joe's work as an Inner City basketball coach and his work with the Roanoke Hawks. According to Pastor Dowell, Joe was well known across the nation for his work with young people. As he got to know him personally, the pastor told him, "Joe, you have a profound God-given talent to reach young people way beyond my capacity to connect with them, and to change their lives. God has prepared you for this ministry."

Pastor Adrian Dowell confers with Deacon Joe Gaither in Shiloh Baptist Church in Salem. Photo by Greg Kiser Photography.

It was clear to the pastor that Joe, who was respected in the congregation, would be a great asset as a member of the board of deacons. After an intense year of required study under the tutelage of Pastor Dowell, which Joe credits with profoundly changing his life, Joe was ordained a deacon in Shiloh Baptist Church. He was not just in the church, but the church was within him. God was not just in the abstract, but his God with whom he conversed. Bernice saw the impact that Pastor Dowell was making in Joe's life through this period. She sums it up with these words, "Joe became the person I fell in love with."

Joe as the extraordinary athlete had known how to win a basketball game. Joe as the coach and mentor had known that to make strong adults, it was about building character through teaching and embodying the values of hard work, sacrifice, honesty, respect, picking oneself up after defeat, teamwork, and aiming higher. Now, Joe as Deacon Gaither easily talked about accessing the power of a greater force and living a life with a greater purpose in mind. So he began including in his team warm-ups Bible verses like: "If God is for you, who can be against you" (Romans 8:31). "To whom much is given, much is required" (Luke 12:48). "Trust in the Lord with all your heart and lean not to your own understanding. In all ways acknowledge Him and He shall direct your path" (Proverbs 3:5).

During his time with the Celtics, Joe recalls one of his players whose parents came to every game. While the mother was extremely friendly, waving at Joe from the stands, the father just scowled. The dad's behavior was so belligerent that it was hard to ignore. Embarrassed at his father's behavior, the young man told his coach, "My Dad has a race problem. He does not like Black people." Joe replied, "I guess I can understand that. I don't like all Black people myself."

Sometime later, the boy's father was in the hospital, critically ill. Joe asked the son if he could visit his father in the hospital and pray with him. The son checked it out with his dad and told his coach that a visit would be okay. So, Joe went to the father's room, talked a bit, and then held the man's hand while Joe led them in prayer. After the prayer ended, the father looked Joe in the eye, pointed at him, and

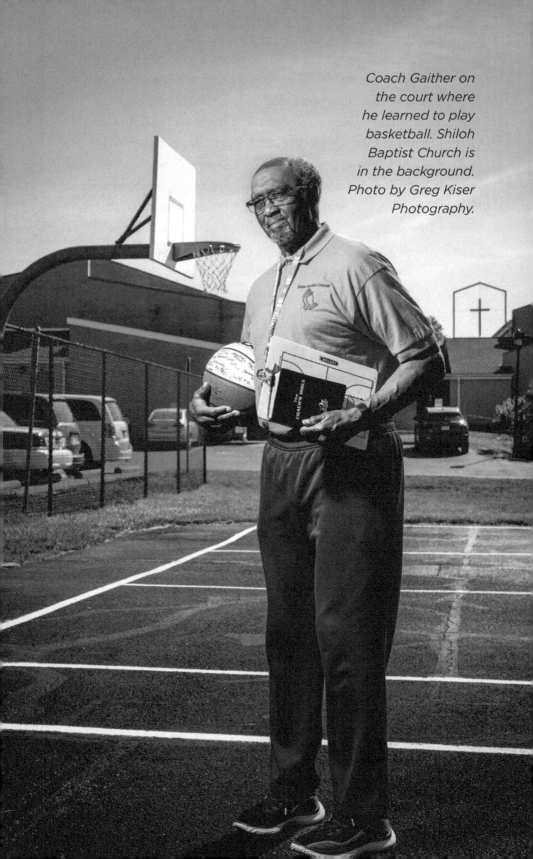

Coach Gaither on the court where he learned to play basketball. Shiloh Baptist Church is in the background. Photo by Greg Kiser Photography.

gave a thumbs-up. A few days later, the boy's father died. Perhaps this is what Martin Luther King Jr. meant when he insisted that the way to overcome hatred is through love.

Reflecting on the many highlights of Joe's incredible career—including his coaching the first basketball team for the ICAA; the William Fleming JV boys' basketball ten-year shutout of Patrick Henry; the Roanoke Hawks' 17 state titles and AAU national final game; and ten years of combined coaching at Roanoke Catholic and Virginia Episcopal School with a total of six state championships—perhaps the success that touches a place most deep in this man is the moment a player finds Jesus as the doorway to the fullness of life.

In response to Joe's question at the end of a VES season—"What did you learn from this season, beyond basketball?"—player Jason Cho (#40) answered that the wealth of his experience, the incredible bond with teammates from a "great mixture of nationalities and personalities," was too great to have been an accidental phenomenon. "There must be God up there, putting all the puzzles together." It was more than just a game, it was "a mission." He concluded, "As we followed the same goal, the bond between the teammates became stronger and stronger. I told in front of everyone that I had been an atheist. But after being part of this team, I became a believer." The next day, Joe reconnected with Jason, and later participated in the young man's baptism.

The great Christian theologian of the twentieth century, Paul Tillich, said that man is beset by three sources of anxiety: the anxiety of life on this earth coming to an end, the anxiety of moral failure, and the anxiety of a meaningless life. The freedom from that anxiety in Christianity is confidence in life beyond death; of forgiveness for misdeeds; and the meaning which comes from living, not just for self, but for others.[17] Jason Cho had moved beyond basketball to the bigger human contest, with which all have to deal. Being with Jason in that moment was Joe's most cherished memory from that season.

---

17   Tillich, Paul. *The Courage to Be*. Yale University Press, 1952.

Joe's ministry was not reserved just to the players he coached. It also extended to his colleagues. One evening after a long practice, Joe and his assistant coach Pat were the last guys to leave the Roanoke Catholic gym. Though he is a gregarious person and a successful businessman, Pat had battled periodic episodes of depression for years, like so many others. This evening was at the end of a stretch of several bad days, and he was exhausted and very down. He and Joe had not known each other for long, so he was reluctant to share his feelings. Joe, however, sensed that his new friend was in a dark place. He told Pat he could tell something was wrong and asked if he could pray with him. Joe's insight and compassion touched Pat, so he agreed, even though he was not particularly religious at the time. Pat recalls:

> Joe took my hands in his and began to pray for my comfort and healing. I could feel the warmth in his hands, and he told me I just needed to accept God's healing grace and let my troubles go. I don't know how to say this except that I left that gym feeling that a tremendous weight had been lifted off me. When I walked through the door that night, my wife even commented that she thought I looked like I felt much better. Though I still have some bad days, I can honestly say that I have never been back to that dark, hopeless place I was before Joe prayed with me. I've seen him do this many times since then with others over the years, and I can tell you with certainty that Joe is a true natural healer. His faith and caring are so deep and real that it seems to transfer to others.

The process of Christian transformation is one that embraces both justification and sanctification. God in Christ, through his life and death, brings us forgiveness for our past failings, and reconnects us with our maker through our faith and trust that God has done this for us. Through God's efforts, we are once again his children and under his eternal protection.

At the same time, we have work to do to become more Christ-like. We are called to focus more on attending to our own failings and focus less on criticizing the inadequacies of others. We are called to evaluate our checkbook and calendar, and direct more of our wealth, money, and time toward those in need, at the sacrifice of investing unnecessary dollars and time in things and activities we can well do without. We are called not to react in kind when others seek to attack us physically, verbally, or through social alienation. Instead, we are called to forgive those who seek to do us harm. This is the process of sanctification in which we take action, with the help of God's power, to grow in grace and exemplify our Savior.

The process of Christian growth is supported by others on the Christian path. They become real life exemplars of faith and growth to help us in our own Christian development.

Such was the case on June 17, 2015, in Charleston, South Carolina, when parishioners had assembled for Bible study at the historic Mother Emanuel Church, founded in 1816. A young White man, Dylan Roof, joined the Black congregants as they gathered to discern God's word for their lives through the Scripture. As they bowed their heads in prayer, the young man drew his gun. He proceeded to shoot and kill nine of the Black congregants. The victims included the senior pastor, a state senator, a doctor, and six others. The killer was arrested and brought to trial. He was convicted of the hate crime murders and sentenced to life imprisonment.

At the trial, the judge allowed family members of those who had been slaughtered to speak. Ethel Lance, the daughter of Nadine Collier, rose to speak. She let her gaze fall and linger on the assassin. Measuring her words, she said, "I will never talk to my mother again. I will never be able to hold her again. But I forgive you. May God have mercy on your soul."[18]

Ms. Lance spoke not just for herself, but also on behalf of others whose loved ones were killed that day. In an America whose history has been laced with racial disdain, fear, and hate since its foundation

---

18 Berman, Mark. "'I Forgive You.' Relatives of Charleston Church Shooting Victims Address Dylann Roof." The Washington Post, October 26, 2021. https://www.washingtonpost.com/news/post-nation/wp/2015/06/19/i-forgive-you-relatives-of-charleston-church-victims-address-dylann-roof/.

and who has witnessed a recent uptick of that poison, an offering of forgiveness to this killer was totally unexpected.

Ethel Lance's response to the man who had so callously brought death and destruction to her life was so unusual that the shock of her words left hearers stunned and speechless. For Joe, it was an example of Christian transformation, a seldom-displayed reaction to horror only made possible by the love of God and the power of the Holy Spirit.

Not long after, Joe and Bernice traveled to Charleston to witness for themselves the site of this tragedy and miracle of faith. As they approached the church, they happened to meet a gentleman who shared that he was a relative of Suzie Jackson, one of the nine who had been killed. The blessing of this personal contact with one so close to what had taken place made the transformative power of God that much more real.

Today, Joe also serves the Shiloh congregation as president of the church's men's ministry. In addition, Deacon Gaither has hosted a golf tournament for the last ten years to raise funds for individuals in need in the Roanoke Valley. The tournament draws around 33 four-person teams to participate each year, raising important resources to improve the lives of fellow citizens.

Over the last seven years, Deacon Gaither has also been an active member of the Fellowship of Christian Athletes. He is frequently called on to play a role in the organization's meetings. Offering a prayer before game time in a team huddle or a prayer after a tough workout was commonplace for Joe. However, offering a prayer before an audience of 600 at a fellowship event featuring a presentation by the famous professional football coach Joe Gibbs was one of those experiences that Joe had previously never imagined as possible.

*Coach Gaither on the court
behind Shiloh Baptist Church.
Photo by Greg Kiser Photography.*

LIFETIME AWARDS

Joe Gaither is a humble man. He is quick to talk about the accomplishments of his players and their teams but downplays his own contributions. His mission in life was never to win awards for himself or collect personal honors—it has always been to help the young men whom he mentored and coached attain recognition beyond what they previously thought was possible. Nevertheless, what he has accomplished has not escaped public notice. Here are a few of the honors William Joseph Gaither has received in recognition of his service to others:

1988 WSET Channel 13 – Jefferson Award for Public Service

1988 Omega Psi Phi Fraternity Citizen of the Year Award

1992 City of Roanoke – Citizen of the Year Award

1992 WDBJ Channel 7 – Hometown Hero Award

1992 Shiloh Baptist Church – Father of the Year Award

1993 U.S. Postal Service of the Year Award

1998 Links, Inc. – Volunteer of the Year Award

2002 Sheiks Athletic Club – Hall of Fame Inductee

2005 U.S. Postal Appalachian District – Diversity Award

2005 Bob Gibbons Tournament of Champions –
Sportsmanship Award

2006 Southern Christian Leadership Conference –
Dr. Martin Luther King Jr. Drum Major for Justice Award

2006/2007 Virginia Independent Schools Athletic Association –
Division II Basketball Coach of the Year Award
2007 Links, Inc. – Citizen of the Year Award

Ironically, it seems the only award that this "power broker,"
who has enriched the lives of countless others, has not won in the
Roanoke Valley is from the Roanoke Chamber of Commerce. This
is the organization that champions those who increase the wealth
of our community through their time and talent, making things of
greater value from what is already available. Joe is not an incorporated
business, but he has been in the business of increasing the self-worth of
youth in our community for decades—the return on investment of his
time and commitment is truly immeasurable.

Then again, perhaps there is still time. When Joe's oldest boy,
Michael, was asked why he was interested in this biography, he said, "I
want to see my dad receive the recognition that he deserves for what he
has contributed to the Roanoke Valley community."

Joe has a place in his home that houses all the trophies that his
teams have won over his four-decade coaching career and the plaques
that have recognized his accomplishments. When asked about his
personal achievements, Joe is quick to say that none of this would have
been possible without his wife and partner, Bernice. With 51 years of
marriage in the books, Bernice has literally been at his side throughout
his whole career. The coach and deacon sums it up: "Like all things in
sport and life, winning is always a team effort."

To that Bernice adds, "Amen."

Coach Joe in his trophy room. Photo by Vincent Willis.

For Joe Gaither, the ultimate contest in life is not on the basketball court. It is winning the race of faith on the track of life without faltering. It is picking yourself up if you fall. And, when crossing the finish line, it is hearing the words, "Well done, my good and faithful servant."

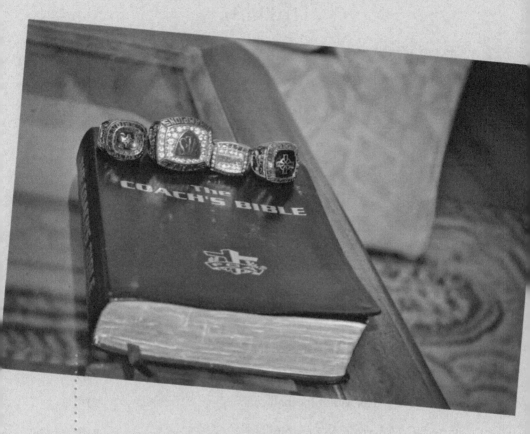

Coach Joe's championship rings and his Coach's Bible.
Photo by Vincent Willis.

THE COACH GAITHER STORY TIMELINE

Cameroon ancestors enslaved and brought to America	1772
Birth of Joe's grandfather, George Holland	1892
Birth of Joe's mother, Laura Holland	1927
Joe's Birth	1949
Graduation from Andrew Lewis High School	1967
Marriage to Bernice Fitzgerald	1970
Drafted in Vietnam War	1970
Served in the U.S. Army in Germany	1970-1972
Birth of son Michael	1971
Returned home from war	1972
Birth of son James	1974
Graduated from Virginia Western Community College	1977
Joined ICAA as assistant football coach	1979
Started ICAA basketball program	1980
Roanoke Hawks AAU Head Coach	1984-1992
William Fleming High School JV Coach	1990-2003
Installed as Deacon of Shiloh Baptist Church	1998
Roanoke Catholic Schools Head Coach	2004-2011
Virginia Episcopal School Associate Coach	2011-2019

AFTERWORD

First and foremost, I give honor to my Lord and Savior, Jesus Christ, for the great things he has done in my life. He is truly the author and finisher of my faith and has demonstrated, "But by the grace of God, I am what I am" (I Corinthians 15:10).

I give honor to my mother, Mrs. Laura Holland Gaither, who 72 years ago gave birth to me and nurtured me, talked to me about God, and then talked to God about me. She was a woman of strength, determination, and endurance. She overcame many obstacles thrown her way. She provided for my every need, often working two jobs and countless hours. She gave me a strong work ethic and always emphasized treating people right, working for what you get. I love you and miss you every day.

I thank God for my beautiful wife, Bernice Fitzgerald Gaither, a Christian woman who has stood beside me through 52 years of marriage. She's been an awesome mother to our sons, Michael and James. She has been my strongest advocate and my strongest critic when I was wrong. She traveled throughout the United States with my AAU teams, prepared meals, made rooming arrangements, washed uniforms, and sometimes drove the vans. She has supported my ministry of coaching young men for these 40-plus years and never complained about my time away from home. Without the love and support of this woman of God, none of this would have been possible. God continues to keep us in a one-accord spirit in this life journey.

I am grateful for my sons, James K. and Michael J. They have made us proud of the men they have become. May God continue to give them favor and draw them even closer to Him. Thank God for my

Michael and James Gaither. Photo by Bernice Gaither.

granddaughter Arianna. We are so proud of her for graduating from Virginia Tech and teaching in Virginia Beach.

I honor my mother- and father-in-law, Mrs. Lucy and Mr. McKinley Fitzgerald, who adopted me into the family as a teenager and loved on me like one of their own. God has called them home to Glory. They are sorely missed.

I honor my pastor and spiritual mentor, Reverend Adrian E. Dowell, who has challenged me to become a man of God. His leadership, teaching, friendship, and preaching have truly transformed my life to be all that God has decreed for my life for the past 28 years. He has not only taught the word of God, he has modeled it through his Christian example.

I give honor to my brother in Christ, William "Boo" Pannell, who has been my right hand in the coaching ministry through the years in the Inner City Athletic Association, at William Fleming, and with the Roanoke Hawks AAU program. He and his wife, Louise, are special people in my life.

I acknowledge Mr. Paul "Creedy" Moyer, who started me out in the coaching ministry at the Inner City Athletic Association. I learned so much from Coach Creedy about the importance of expecting and demanding the best from young people, respecting authority, and loving God.

I am so grateful to Barry Brown, a former coworker who birthed the idea of this book project and was the driving force behind it. I will always appreciate the time and energy he devoted to research, interviews, and photoshoots. God's blessings to you and your family!

I am thankful to my longtime friend Ted Edlich, who has been a constant supporter of every endeavor I have undertaken through my years at the Inner City Athletic Association. He helped me form and facilitate the Roanoke Hawks AAU basketball program. Your countless, tireless efforts to tell the story of my life will always be gratefully appreciated. You have encouraged me for many years. I love you much.

I want to acknowledge my good friend Steve Bowery, who has been a confidant, fundraiser, and one of my closest friends over the years. Thank you, Steve, for always believing in my vision for Roanoke's youth and helping us travel all over the USA, showcasing their talents and enhancing their college opportunities. Blessings to you and Joy!

I want to thank the parents of all the athletes who have played for me over the years. You trusted me to teach, mentor, coach, and sometimes discipline your children. You allowed me to bring out the best in them through the athletic arenas. I hope I deposited something in their spirits to help them become better men.

To all the young men who ever played for "Coach Joe": I thank God for enhancing my life through you all, for challenging me to give you my best to help you become your best. I have fond memories and love in my heart for each one of you. I pray that I have been an example to each of you of the grace of God. I hope that the scripture I always shared with you will continue to stay in your heart. "To whom much is given, much is required" (Luke 12:48). As you move in each stage in your life, remember the words of Paul in Colossians 3:17: "And whatever you do in word or deed, do all in the name of the Lord Jesus."

Finally, to my longtime friend Dave Russo, thank you for becoming a huge part of this team of writers and bringing this project to fruition. You and your family have been there for my mom and me from the beginning of our days in Salem. Much love to you and the Russo family, who helped us through the rough times. Blessings to you and Lila.

-Joe Gaither

ACKNOWLEDGEMENTS

For 40 years, I was the president and CEO of Total Action Against Poverty (TAP), a nonprofit organization in the Roanoke Valley of southwest Virginia. As a Community Action Agency, one of TAP's earliest strategies was to work for change by supporting the efforts of area residents to improve the conditions of life in their neighborhoods.

In the late 1970s, I learned about the work of the Inner City Athletic Association, which was formed to promote sandlot athletics as a way to teach youngsters traits that would make them winners on the athletic field, in their classrooms, and anywhere they might go for the rest of their lives.

That's how I first met Joe Gaither. Over the following half-century, I watched in awe as he played a pivotal role in advancing the lives of hundreds, if not thousands, of young men—many from some of our poorest neighborhoods—through the medium of athletics.

His curriculum: Out-work your opposition. Push yourself to be better. Place the team win above personal ambitions. Believe in a power greater than yourself that is on your side. Test yourself against the best. At all times, respect others.

Among his protégés are top athletes who have been NCAA basketball and football standouts, those who have played for professional NFL and NBA teams, and many who have coached at the high school, college, and professional levels. Scores more have earned a college degree, become contributing members of society, and passed lessons learned to their children.

Joe's story is one of the power of voluntary giving, a distinctive

American quality first identified by Alexis de Tocqueville's study of America in 1831. After his service in the Vietnam War, Joe worked most of his life as an employee of the U.S. Post Office. Most of his coaching was done as a volunteer or a second job. Yet, his first-class talent and contributions are well-known to many in the professional athletic coaching business.

The Joe Gaither story is one that begged to be told. Nevertheless, it may never have been put to paper had it not been for the inspiration of Barry Brown to put the idea forward, secure Joe's agreement to the project, and do the initial research that validated that this was a popular idea and that others were willing to contribute their testimonies.

It has been my privilege to work with Barry and Joe and to lend my writing abilities to the development of this manuscript. While I know there are writers with far more talent, I am pleased that Joe feels that we have accurately captured the critical moments of his life, the sources of his strength, and the description of his untiring mission to serve others with his very special skill set.

I am compelled to acknowledge the important contributions of all persons that I have been privileged to interview for this work. A special shout out to Joe and Bernice Gaither, Michael Gaither, Pastor Adrian Dowell, and businessman Steve Bowery. I also owe a special debt to several athletes who trained under Coach Joe—at various stages of their lives and his career—for sharing their personal reflections. These include Curtis Staples, Curtis Blair, George Lynch, Shannon Taylor, Eugene Cook, Russell Turner, Tony Joyce, Kalleone Moret, and Jermaine Hardy. The interview contributions of fellow coaches Pat King and William Pannell have also been immensely helpful in the telling of *The Coach Gaither Story*.

Behind every person, there is a family. Behind every family, there are ancestors who have been shaped by a particular history. To ignore those people, that history, is to ignore the landscape that shapes life and the context that ultimately fashions each individual person. Roland Lazenby's book, *Michael Jordan: The Life*, demonstrates the power of including the story of one's forbearers as helping to define an individual biography and its place in history. Roland, thank you for this valuable insight.

Slavery is an acid that too often has erased noble ancestries from Americans with black skin in this country. The message sent to those enslaved and their ancestors is, "Not only are you a nobody, you are a nobody with a contribution-less past that is not worth telling or even remembering!"

Thus, I am deeply grateful for the extensive historical research undertaken by Joe's cousin, William Holland, into the family's ancestral African roots. I have restricted reference to this research to information available in the public domain through published articles. I can only hope that Mr. Holland and his family will publish their full findings, so that this information is available to the public at a future date.

Once again, I am thankful for the professional ear and eye of Emily Kincer, my editor, whose mastery of the English language always transforms my sentences into what I really wanted to say and, more often, what I should have said, and how I should have said it in the first place. Thank you so much. All of us who have contributed to this book are indebted to you for your investment in this project.

Barry originally envisioned a comprehensive biography on the life of Joe Gaither. Frankly, we soon discovered that such an effort is beyond the available resources devoted to this work. Those interviewed are but a small percentage of more than 100 people whose reflections would have made this a richer document.

What we do have is a biographical sketch of Joe's life. Nevertheless, it is our hope that within the limitation of space and content, this document still accurately reflects the life of this great man, whom we have come to know and love. Our hope is that this book will encourage others to enlarge this story in print or film for a much larger audience.

Finally, I want to acknowledge my deep appreciation to Dave Russo, whose own story is woven into the life of Joe Gaither and Laura, Joe's mother. Dave's personal reflections have helped this story immensely, and he has further enriched the manuscript through his interviews with key contributors. Furthermore, his willingness to take this manuscript and turn it into a published volume is most welcomed. Dave, thank you for your leadership in this venture.

Barry and I gratefully contribute the full copyright authority over *The Coach Gaither Story* to William Joseph Gaither. For both of us, this has been a labor of love. Joe, thank you for trusting us.

–Ted Edlich

AUTHOR BIOS

TED EDLICH is the lead writer for *The Coach Gaither Story*. He has been Joe Gaither's friend and collaborator in Roanoke youth sports for over forty years. He took inspiration from Barry Brown's ideas and drafts and developed the story into what it is today.

Ted was the President and CEO of Total Action for Progress from 1975 to 2015. He's the author of *Navigating the Nonprofit Rapids: Strategies* and *Tactics for Running a Nonprofit Company*, 2016.

Ted has an undergraduate degree in history from UNC, graduate degrees from Union Theological Seminary in Richmond and Yale Divinity School, and an Honorary Doctor of Letters from Washington and Lee University.

BARRY BROWN is a first-time contributing author of *The Coach Gaither Story*. If not for Barry, this story might not have been told.

A sports nut by nature, Barry presented the idea of a book to Joe after hearing so many wonderful tales about Joe's years of coaching youth basketball and the young men he mentored along the way. He secured Joe's agreement for the project. He validated that a book about Joe was a popular idea and that many people were willing to tell their part of the story.

Barry is a 21-year veteran of the United States Army, now retired. When not working on his degree in Health and Physical Education, he enjoys spending time with his beautiful wife and coaching his young son, Hayden, in various sports.

Barry is a 1988 graduate of Staunton River School, where he lettered in basketball, football, and track. He lives in Roanoke, Virginia, but plans to move to the Philippines, his wife's home country, where the family can bask in the Philippine climate.

DAVE RUSSO is the consulting editor for *The Coach Gaither Story*. He shares more than a little history with Joe Gaither and his mother, Laura Gaither. It is the privilege of a lifetime for him to help bring this story to life.

Dave is a retired technical writer who worked for SAS, an analytics software company. He has an undergraduate degree in English from Roanoke College and an M.F.A from the University of Iowa.

Made in the USA
Columbia, SC
31 July 2022

64387279R00070